WHAT AILS OUR SCHOOLS?

WHAT AILS OUR SCHOOLS?

Vimala Nandakumar

PARTRIDGE

A Penguin Company

Partridge books may be ordered through booksellers or by contacting:

Partridge India
Penguin Books India Pvt.Ltd
11, Community Centre, Panchsheel Park, New Delhi 110017
India
www.partridgepublishing.com
Phone: 000.800.10062.62

Dedicated to
My fantastic Students who mean the world to me
and
The entire student community of our country

ACKNOWLEDGEMENT

I am thankful eternally to my parents who made sacrifices to educate me. It is entirely due to them that I reached peaks in my career—each one higher than the previous. I seek their blessings, wherever they are!

I thank my husband, Nandakumar, my son, Aditya and his wife, Divya, for the encouragement and support I received from them. I acknowledge that it is due to their continuous monitoring that I could make progress with the book.

I am thankful to my brother, Ravi Shanker alias Avalok Sastry, for his fantastic cover photograph.

Ms Tarana Pithawala is a well known clinical psychologist. Her approach is student-centric. Her views on students and what should be done to improve the lot of the students in the schools are valuable. I am indebted to Ms Tarana Pithawala for agreeing to write the foreword to this book.

I am pleased to acknowledge the efforts taken by my former students, Nirmal Balaraman, Sandeep Bajaj, Nandakumar Prabhakaran, Vanama Radhika and Latha Sampath to write the piece entitled, "Read on . . ."

I wish to record my gratitude to Vijay D'Costa for giving life to the book by his illustrations. His ability to capture the moods of the characters of the book makes him a special artist we rarely come across. I am grateful to him for the extraordinary efforts he took and the grace with which he completed all the illustrations within the specified time line.

I thank Pritesh Rao, a truly professional photographer for making time for my photo shoot through his busy schedule.

Lastly and most importantly I must thank all my students, friends, colleagues, principals, trustees, the administrative and the support staff of every school where I worked for inspiring me to write this book.

Vimala Nandakumar
Navi Mumbai

FOREWORD

Those who educate children well are more to be honoured than they who produce them; for these only gave them life, those the art of living well—Aristotle

As a student I have always looked up to my teachers with admiration and fondness. I decided I wanted to be a teacher in my second standard, and I did follow through with that idea! I fondly remember my days at Udayachal School, run by Godrej at Vikhroli. It was a blessing in disguise to all us students as there, we had the freedom to be children. We were exposed to art, culture, yoga, physical education, philosophy, as well as the otherwise classroom subjects in the most creative manner possible. Yes, we did also study under palm trees and learned most things through observation and experimentation. We weren't just well informed in the subjects we were encouraged to think independently about concepts and their application. There was ample time to study, reflect, play and engage in hobbies at leisure in an accepting, non-judgemental environment. A fabulous set of disciplined teachers, an absolutely approachable principal and a wonderful set up. We couldn't have asked for more. Most of us students have selected professions that suit our nature and abilities almost perfectly. When I meet fellow students today, the one thing I cannot miss is a visible firm grounding in values that help us function dynamically and in a spirit of service. I feel grateful for having an education that not just gave me knowledge but enabled me to take up any challenge with enthusiasm, confidence and poise. I hope to pass on what I have imbibed through my work, and through the way I lead my life.

I read a poem once, titled, 'This Child is yours, to Make or Mar'. Parents and teachers are extremely powerful figures in the life of a child. When they raise children with an empathic understanding, unconditional acceptance, in a psychological climate of freedom, to express, to experiment, to toy with ideas, to discuss, to learn, to keep their innate curiosity burning, children grow to be confident, self assured, willing to think and do things differently from the herd, and lead a healthy, happy, dynamic life. Teachers affect us a great deal even long after we have graduated from school, college, university. What they say, what they do, their style of teaching, the strategies they use, their ways of problem solving, their temperament every single aspect influences children and becomes a part of their psyche, of their life. As children, we like/dislike certain subjects, thanks to the teachers who introduced us to them, we believe in our abilities, when they believe in us.

Research studies have concluded that 'the association between the quality of early teacher-student relationships and later school performance can be strong and persistent.' Even children with significant behavioural problems are less likely to face difficulties later if the teachers are sensitive to their needs and use an authoritative style of disciplining (a style characterised by warmth, acceptance, sensitivity to the child's needs, open, assertive communication and disciplining through polite, firm communication and reason).

As a teacher, I realised, preparation is vital. Having a lesson plan in place, knowing the subject really well, not only enhances the teacher's confidence, but enables her to welcome questions and have the flexibility to use different approaches to teaching. It is an essential discipline in order to really draw out the best in students. After all, it is important that as a teacher I not just expose them to the riches I have acquired, but 'to reveal to them their own.' Another vital quality is a good sense of humour. I can never forget the teachers who enjoyed a good joke, who were sporting when we played pranks, who never personalised the healthy '*masti*' we did in school. They were not only loved by all but also obeyed and respected for their maturity. As Carl Jung says, children are educated by what the grown-up is and not by his talk.

As a psychologist, I know there is so much more we can do to better our education system, the quality of and methods in which education is imparted. Right from using the knowledge available to us in the fields of developmental and educational psychology and implementing effective teaching and learning methods to imparting the basics of life, a school has the opportunity to do it all. It is not just the theoretical, technical knowledge that will help our wards progress in life, it is a realistic understanding of themselves and of life itself that will enable them to apply the knowledge we impart. As it were, there is a manual to life, as there is to any new gadget we use. Once we understand the basics, it is easy to operate it and use it without any problems. When we are given the tools of objectivity, concentration, consistency, skill in action and a goal beyond ourselves to focus on, we are able to sail through life without stress or strain.

Three important aspects to focus on in schools from a psychologist's perspective would be to enhance self awareness and acceptance, improve communication skills in order to be more assertive, develop more rational, logical thinking in order to have realistic, flexible expectations from themselves, others and life in general. This combination allows for clarity in thought, happy, disturbance free, focussed action wherein success just follows.

This book is a sincere effort by Ms. Vimala Nandakumar to bring to awareness and bridge the gap between what is and what can be. I have known Ms. Nandakumar in the capacity of a principal as well as an eternal student. A disciplined, elegant lady, with high ideals, yet she has made sure the child in her is alive and energetic. The teachers who have worked with her have only praises for the way she functions as well as the rapport she has with each one of them. She has the best intentions at heart and as an educationist, wants what is best for our children.

Walt Disney was of the opinion that 'crowded classrooms and half-day sessions are a tragic waste of our greatest national resource—the minds of our children.' This book endeavours to make our education system worthy of these young minds. We owe to the child the best we have.

Tarana Pithawalla
Clinical Psychologist, Mumbai

CONTENTS

READ ON . . .

I was lucky. I studied in a school which consistently produced outstanding students. We would have 6-10 students getting into the IITs every year (that is 0.5% of the entire intake at the time I went to school) and many more getting into medical school. We would regularly have students placing in the National Physics and Math Olympiads. Of my graduating class of 50 students in the Electronics stream, 48 became engineers.

Of course, this did not happen by accident. Most of us had highly educated parents. Naturally, education was highly prized and academics encouraged. But the other part of the puzzle was the school itself.

We had some excellent teachers who would go out of the way to educate us (and not just "finish the portion".) My maths teacher in Std. VIII would seem to be rambling about the world in general, but then he would almost obliquely teach us tricks that made mathematical operations simpler and more interesting. I still apply some of his tricks subconsciously and can do multiplications and divisions faster than most people I know. Our principal was so passionate about Mathematics that he had scientists from renowned research institutions give us talks on applying what we learn to Olympiad Math problems. My English teacher in Std. IX once divided our class into four groups. She would call out words, and one group would have to give the noun form of the word, another the verb form, another adjective and the fourth the adverb form. As we competed, we were thinking through rules of English that would otherwise have made for a horrendous lecture.

Mrs. Nandakumar was one of these gifted teachers. I was in her Std. X Math class. I remember the first day of school when, instead of going to the board and writing formulae, she shared her vacation pictures from a trip to North East India. Immediately, she had gained our trust. We had a friend, not a tyrant. One Saturday, when we had a free period towards the end of the day, she challenged us with logic puzzles. These were introduced in such a way that I doubt any of us were upset at not getting to leave early. This was a game we were playing, and the fact that we were learning techniques we could use down the road never struck us.

My classmate, Sandeep, moved to our school from an entirely different curriculum in Std. IX, and was getting overwhelmed by his new surroundings. Mrs. Nandakumar took him under her wing and spent time with him after class to help him get settled in. She was successful to such an extent that Sandeep was the top performer from our school at the Class X and Class XII board exams, and at the IIT JEE.

A couple of years after I graduated, Mrs. Nandakumar invited me back to the school. She had started a Maths Club to encourage students. I attended one of their meetings and spoke of my experience at the Math Olympiad. Mrs. Nandakumar was running the club after school hours on her own time. I was amazed at the thought that had gone into it. How often do you see students voluntarily meeting after school because they are excited to participate in Math-based activities?

This was the only school I knew, and like all kids (and parents, I realize now), I found reasons to nitpick about the school. It was only later, in talking with others, that I realized how different our school was from the norm in India. Most people I meet have stories of classes crammed past capacity and teachers consequently struggling to connect to students. I often hear stories of teachers perfunctorily reading through textbooks, assigning textbook problems as homework and expecting rote answers. While I was appreciated for taking an answer in the opposite direction to that discussed in class in a Std. IX English exam, I have heard many examples of teachers not taking kindly to independent thought.

Much of this is not the fault of individual teachers. If I had to summarize the Indian education system in one phrase, I would say it has perfected mediocrity. It excels in getting a student to mediocrity who might otherwise fail, but it also excels in getting an otherwise brilliant student to mediocrity. Since there is no differentiation of students based on their ability, everybody gets taught at the pace of the average student. We were informed by the education board that no molecules with more than four carbon atoms were allowed in the Std. XII Organic Chemistry exam because some students may get intimidated. We were told at the beginning of the year that the HSC Math exam would have four choices on the first question of which we would have to do two. The four choices would consist of one problem each in limits, continuity and two other topics. Obviously, many just skipped two of the four topics.

Doing well in these exams is very different from learning the subjects they supposedly test. Studying becomes a process of gaining information, not knowledge, and this leaves students ill-equipped to apply learned concepts in real-life situations.

Mrs. Nandakumar has faced these issues both as a teacher and as a principal. As a teacher, she prepared us well to face the exam, but at the same time she also encouraged us to think for ourselves. As a principal, she has faced the peculiar pressures brought about by school boards, parents and students. In the book that follows, she presents her experiences and thoughts on what ails the Indian education system and some prescriptions to improve it, a subject she is extremely qualified to address.

Nirmal Balaraman, with inputs from
Sandeep Bajaj, Nandakumar Prabhakaran,
Vanama Radhika and Latha Sampath

TO BEGIN WITH

The glorious days of Indian history were characterised by the importance accorded to *value-based* education. In the last couple of centuries some countries overtook us in the field of education. The reason is not far to seek. They gave greater importance to education. I hold that we have been left behind despite the fact that India has the largest pool of scientists and engineers. The reason is that we *lost focus on education*.

Pre—and post-independence saw a poverty-ridden and illiterate Indian populace, a huge price that we had to pay for being ruled by foreigners. Education at that time was available only to a fortunate few. The scenario is different now. All of a sudden the government has woken up to the fact that it has the huge challenge of providing education to more than 240 million children. Policies such as 'Every child has a right to education', 'Abolish child labour', 'Mid-day meal', and 'free education to the girl child' are indications that the government has taken education seriously. However, the implementation of these policies leaves a lot to be desired. Even now we are *not focusing on education.*

Educating a huge part of one billion-population is no mean task. Allocation of major funds for education is still not a priority for the government. Changes could be brought about only if this issue is addressed.

In the recent past, the Central Board of Secondary Education (CBSE) made changes in the curriculum and policies related to schools in order to make them student-friendly. Sadly, this resulted in thousands of students being left in the lurch without getting admission to good junior colleges. In order to avoid stress to students of Standard X, the CBSE made board examination optional for them. Consequently only those students who wanted to pursue standard XI in CBSE opted for school-based examinations of standard X. Some of these students changed their minds after passing the school – based examinations of standard X and applied for other boards for their standard XI. They were refused admission since they did not take up the board examination of standard X of CBSE. This led to confusion. CBSE had to back track saying that there were no differences between the board and school-based exams conducted for their standard X students but the other boards refused to buy this argument.

The following excerpts from an article entitled, *Students hold on to board exams*, published in *DNA CITY dated 6 October 2012* give a clear picture of what is happening in schools:

The Board introduced the school-based examinations option two years ago, hoping to reduce exam stress in students. However, students do not seem to be opting for this stress-free choice. Principals say that this is because both parents and students still strongly believe that only board exams hold value. The parents feel that the students will not take internal exams seriously and will be lethargic and not give their best. They choose board exams as many institutions for higher education do not recognise school-based exams. Parents admit that *the concept of holding internal exams is a good one.* However, they do not want their ward's career prospects getting restricted because of it. Further, their children might not get admission into courses abroad, as those institutes might not recognise a 'school-based' exam.

Education can be classified broadly into three categories— for the rich, for the middle class and for the poor. In the past it was only the rich who sent their children to exclusive residential schools. Their wards remained in the world of exclusive class.

The middle class was exposed to a system of education which can be best described as "one-size-fits-all", but because of their desire to reach higher levels, using their intrinsic ability to grasp the nuances of education they benefitted. Probably these students are the lot who made it big in IT, medicine and the corporate world.

The children of impecunious parents were denied access to good quality education. In a poor family, the child would not be sent to school as every additional member of the family contributed to the daily earnings. Therefore, the poor produced more children thereby increasing the number of children who could not be educated. The poor thus got into a vicious circle.

The abolition of child labour and the implementation of RTE have brought in their wake increased awareness among the poor. The lives of the poor have now started showing signs of improvement though to a very limited extent. The recent news about the implementation of the learning guarantee programme (LGP) in 45,000 rural schools in Karnataka is promising. Many NGOs, for example, *Akanksha Foundation, Teach for India, Pratham, Parikrama, Azim Premji Foundation* and *Naandi Foundation*, are doing yeomen service by providing quality education to students of the schools for the underprivileged. Many youngsters have quit lucrative jobs abroad to teach in such institutions in India.

Adoption of international curriculum by schools is a significant forward leap in the field of education. International curricula lay stress on comprehension, application, analysis and developing problem-solving skills rather than rote-learning. Since the international curriculum is impressive, it has resulted in the mushrooming of international schools in every nook and cranny of the cities in India. As the prospects of operating international schools in terms of cash inflow are very attractive, even some people who may have hardly more than a nodding acquaintance with international curriculum have jumped on the bandwagon. Parents who have been in and out of the country feel that a big gap exists between education in India and abroad and do not want to take "risks" with their children's education! They try out new international schools.

Schools, in the name of imparting international curriculum charge higher fees—a practice, which till recently was restricted only to the elite international schools. The middle class families in India recently have become financially sound and want to educate their children in international schools that are affiliated to the University of Cambridge and International Baccalaureate. These international boards of education require enormous infrastructure and training of teachers which is an expensive proposition. The fee charged by the schools offering international curriculum is more than that charged by the schools offering national curricula. Unfortunately the salaries of the teachers and of the Principal of international schools in India are not necessarily "international"!

We have discussed only policies and curricula. Let us take a closer look at schools and the components of schools.

School is an integral part of one's life. One discards the comfort of home and the warmth of mother's hug to set foot on the big wilderness called the outside world as early as at the age of 3. These days it is worse. The child accompanied by the mother attends the "mother-toddler batch" at the age of one year and nine months!

Relationships are built in schools. Friendships are developed, bullies feared and teachers admired in the beginning years. This admiration for teachers slowly turns into respect in the middle schools. In the higher classes one finds some teachers running for cover all the time.

It is a rare teacher who is able to create interest in what he/she teaches in higher classes. Mostly students enjoy fooling teachers and totally lose any respect for them unless the teacher is extraordinary.

It is not as if there are no ideal teachers. Because of the way schools are run, *talented teachers find it difficult to work.* Many *teachers leave schools if they are not given freedom to innovate.* Substandard work culture ruins the chances of retaining good teachers in schools. A teacher is rarely given an opportunity to make suggestions to improve the school's functioning. It leads to clash of ego. The school management does not care if a good teacher leaves because there are many teachers of uncertain standards available in the job market! The quality gets compromised.

The teaching profession does not attract the best talent. Schools are lucky if they get good teachers who show loyalty to the school and stick to the school for long. Teachers' pay is low as is their status in the society.

There appears to be gender bias towards this profession. This fact came to the fore in a conference held in Kolkatta. At the conference, all the speakers on the dais were men. They criticised school teachers and Principals for "ruining" the lives of students. They said that Principals were hardly seen by the students and that teachers were insensitive to the needs of students and insincere to the profession. They made many more negative remarks about teachers and Principals. They were making sweeping remarks on the hapless teaching professionals. They were manifestly contradicted by the sincerity with which the audience, consisting almost entirely of ladies, was taking notes.

During the Q & A session, I specifically addressed those speakers who had made caustic remarks on teachers and said "Please note that the audience is busy taking notes of what is being said. They are all lady teachers. The audience wants to implement the newer methods suggested by you in the classes. Just why don't men join schools as teachers to make a difference to students?"

There was a deafening silence everywhere. Speakers then in reply mumbled that the salaries of teachers were low and their status was low as well!

There is scope for improvement in schools. Achieving excellence should be the motto of those who are responsible for imparting education. In India, women are burdened with the lion's share of domestic responsibilities. It would appear that men do not perceive much dignity in being school teachers. If they overcome this bias and enter the arena, the perception about the status of teachers would improve. Better salaries would follow. More male teachers in schools would provide a proper balance to the profession.

The pages you are going to read are about the elements of a school, namely, parents, teachers, Principals, management, and most importantly students. Often students' misbehaviour gets highlighted. Of all these, *the misbehaviour of students, is the easiest to manage* provided such misbehaviour is devoid of the influence of others. Left to themselves the students are clear in their minds about what is right and what is wrong. Most of the time, they are tempted to test the environment to check if they can choose what is suitable to them. They are, after all mini adults! They only need a strong mentor to assure them that the right path is the best one to choose and then they immediately fall in line *provided the mentor leads by example*. They want to be heard, spoken up to and not talked down. *They are the best part of schools and for them the school days are the best.* Should the schools not keep focus on them all the time? Don't they need the best of facilities, teachers and quality education? Are the students the only ones who misbehave? Are parents, teachers, Principals and management doing everything they should for maintaining / improving school educational standards in India?

Some schools focus only on academics, some on only co-curricular and some on neither. Some schools go overboard and allow themselves to be run by parents.

This book is based on what I learnt from my experience in the teaching profession spanning four decades and from many others. It includes anecdotes and case studies collected while teaching in schools and Junior Colleges in India and abroad.

The reader who may be a Principal or a Teacher or a Parent or a management trustee may not agree with certain views expressed in this book. I appeal to the reader to see things from the viewpoint of the student to appreciate what is said in this book.

This **book gives due credit** to managements, Principals, Teachers and Parents for their actions in the interest of the students.

This book *portrays different colours of which the fabric of school is made. The colours of fabrics are different in different schools but the texture, namely, the students, is much the same.*

Students are at the focus of this book.

CHAPTER 1
INTRODUCTION

Quality of education

I started exploring the job market in 1977 not without trepidation as I was very sceptical about entering the teaching profession. I even let go of an opportunity to join a B.Ed. college. However, I joined the B.Ed. course many years later thanks to the encouragement that I received from one of my friends. Before joining the B.Ed. course, I had secured a couple of leave vacancy jobs in schools. I realized, to my amazement, the true "direction" of teaching only when I actually did the B.Ed. course. Normally almost everyone scoffs at the course as being out-dated and even irrelevant as it is not in tune with changing times. I partially agree with them but I would not like to throw the baby with the bath water. The guidance provided by educationists and philosophers continues to be relevant even today. However, the method of implementation of the guidance has to be updated. After I completed the B.Ed. course my scepticism about entering the teaching profession vanished as I realized that my passion lay in this field. My love for children made me decide in favour of teaching.

Armed with the B.Ed. degree it was easy to get a job. Ironically at the time of interview, the first question that they would ask would be, "Have you done B.Ed.?" Within a few months the same individuals would earnestly advise one, "Don't follow the B.Ed. methods. You won't be able to complete the syllabus." Teachers should, in fact, be encouraged to use what they learnt in the B.Ed. course.

We read about Indian students performing impressively in foreign universities. Indian students do well in SpellBee contests, SAT and International Olympiads. India has the largest number of qualified scientists and engineers in the world. Indians are readily employed all over the world. They shine in the IT field. All this does not mean that our educational system is the best in the world. These achievers form a miniscule fraction of the students from India and they could do what they have done entirely because of their own efforts, parental support and opportunities in addition to any support that they might have got from their school. The rest of the Indian students who are left behind despite having the same or even greater potential could have done better if the educational system had supported them adequately.

An article by Shubangi Khapre published in the newspaper, DNA, dated 7 March 2011 reinforces the thought. A Rajya Sabha member demanded that IIT entrance exams be conducted in regional languages as well. Evidently, the real barrier is not the English language but the declining standards of teaching maths and science in government schools. This being the reality, preparing the students for competitive exams remains out of the question. Even the policy of the IITs to open branches in Roorkee and Guwahati for regional balance has not helped much. IIT is still a distant dream for students from villages and small towns. (DNA 21/03/11).

Educating a large number of children is the responsibility of the state. The pathetic condition of school children in

India is illustrated in an article entitled *Brick in the wall* that appeared in the *Times of India* dated 18 January 2012 summarised below:

A survey of the Quality of Education in high-end schools in metropolitan cities found them lacking in quality parameters and indicted them for excessive reliance on rote learning.

A programme conducted by OECD (Organisation for Economic Co-operation and Development) for International student Assessment ranked Indian higher secondary students only better than those from Kyrgzstan among 74 participating countries.

Pratham's Annual Status of Education Report (ASER), 2011, assessing schools in rural India, found declining attendance, over-reliance on private tuitions and declining reading and mathematical abilities of children in the 6 to 14 years age category.

Despite a welcome high enrolment rate of about 96.7% at the primary and upper primary levels, the quality of school learning is simply not up to the mark. Most of the government schools lack basic infrastructure such as black boards and text books. Teaching standards are poor, with higher teacher absenteeism. Only 48.2% of class V students surveyed under ASER were able to read class II-level texts. There were other depressing statistics.

The Right To Education (RTE) Act, with its objective of providing free and compulsory education to all primary school children, misses the quality issue. Meanwhile, by imposing strict parameters on private schools, the RTE has squeezed the few entrepreneurs engaged in this field, disincentivising further investment.

Issues of quality can only be addressed by raising the standards of public schools. This can be done by ensuring that they have enough resources and introducing better pedagogy as well as over sight of teaching staff, so that pay and promotion are linked to performance.

So much for the quality of education in schools! There is another matter that is a cause for serious concern.

Discrimination of students

Schools differentiate between students of different strata. All children want to be taught by good teachers. They want to learn and to get their doubts cleared but often their voices are smothered.

A report that appeared in The Hindu on 11th July 2011 was shocking. In the rural areas of India a single teacher handles four classes at the same time. Many states accord importance to providing education to the underprivileged but in practice it does not happen.

Dalit students carry their own plates to school for having the lunch provided by the school. ***Untouchability still exists in the land of the Mahatma!***

This book . . .

I have compiled my experience in the field of education in this book. *I am not naming any school because it is irrelevant.* What is relevant is to identify / recognize the common malaise in the teaching profession and seek workable solutions. These solutions could be complex and implementing them could be a huge challenge. Few acknowledge the malaise and are willing to address these challenges. The various pillars of the edifice of education such as school authorities, teachers, teacher trainers, text-book writers and curriculum developers are working in a disjointed manner. This has resulted in various ailments that afflict our schools. The negative consequence is faced by students.

The instances discussed in this book involve students directly or indirectly.

The very purpose of educating the young minds is defeated by the failure of the educational institutions to live up to good standards. In spite of the incoherence among the institutions, *it is to the credit of the students that they manage to get educated in our schools.*

This book applauds the efforts of those teachers, Principals, support staff for whom children come first. Unfortunately if the total number of people working in a school is N, the good workers would number only a small fraction of N. This is obviously not enough considering the huge population waiting and wanting to be educated.

Here is an attempt to provide a sampling of some of the problems that plague the educational system in our country.

It is necessary to bring it before the readers because the reader could be a teacher or a Principal or a member of the school management or a parent or a student. It concerns all of us, whatever role we play in the education system.

The presentation of the facts in this book could be influenced by my perception though I have tried to avoid subjectivity in the discussions. The episodes discussed herein bring into focus some of the important concerns. The narration of the episodes is not entirely autobiographical because the contents reflect not merely my experience but also what others in this profession go through.

I am not pointing a finger at any individual or organization. I found both good and not-so-good aspects in schools. I have mentioned only the imperfections not because there are only imperfections in our system but because these are areas that need to be remedied urgently. I am certainly not trying to thrust my views on the reader.

I have respect for the readers' judgement.

CHAPTER 2
GOOD TEACHERS

Qualification is necessary for any profession. Teaching is no exception. The treatment given to a qualified teacher is very different from that given to one who is not even if the latter has the talent and natural inclination to teach. A person without a teacher's qualification has to take a bit of trouble to get a temporary teaching job. Neither the students nor the other teachers take her seriously. She is there only as a temporary hand, like the twelfth man or a substitute fielder in a cricket team!

A person who is not a B.Ed. may be taken to fill a temporary vacancy. It happened in my case. In 1977, I ventured into the teaching profession for the first time in a school far away from my residence. A consolidated salary of Rs. 450/= was promised in the appointment letter. To earn this munificence I had to travel from my residence at 5:30 in the morning, change two buses and walk about 2 km through narrow crowded dirty streets to reach the school on time.

At the school I wanted to teach the students to the best of my ability but *the school did not expect anything of a temporary teacher!* The management only wanted a baby-sitter for the students for a few months and the students too looked upon the new teacher as one. The colleagues were amused that I took my job seriously. The other teachers did not seem to be troubling themselves to teach any too well. It was overall an exploitative situation where everyone exploited everyone else and did not feel guilty about it. *The students who were supposed to have been the focus were simply pushed to the background.*

Subsequently, I was employed as a teacher to fill a temporary vacancy in a relatively high profile school where the Principal was described by the school staff as a tyrant. There was an environment of fear in the staff room which was beset with group-ism. It was known that the place was abounding in spies in the form of teachers and students. Therefore, truth was dealt at a premium. The staff members consisted of just a few permanent employees and a disproportionately large number of temporary staff. This was by design.

Temporary teachers are targets of easy exploitation. Their salary is low. They actually support the permanent staff members. However, if there is a strike, it is the temporary teachers who would be sacrificed. Many years ago, there was of a month-long strike in schools called by the teachers who were permanent employees. Though the schools were any way not functioning during the strike the temporary teachers were deemed to have "joined the strike". After the strike failed, the teachers – both temporary and permanent— were asked to teach extra hours to cover the lost portion which was fair as far as the students were concerned. The permanent teachers were paid their salaries for the strike period whereas the temporary teachers were not. This differential treatment meted out to teachers is not considered unacceptable by any one. Sadly the teachers have become immune to such treatment.

Salaries of teachers are very low even now. A report in the Times of India dated September 3, 2011 states the facts, as given in the table below.

Profession	Earnings per month (Rs)
Chauffeurs	8000-15,000
Domestic helps	3000-6000
Nannies	4000-8000
Autorickshaw drivers	6000-12000

Here is an extract from the report:

"A salary of Rs 4000 would not attract the best talent to teaching in Mumbai, where a room in the slums will cost many times more. Our policy—makers need to revise their priorities to ensure that those instilling values and life skills in kids get paid an amount they would not be ashamed of revealing. We owe it to the next generation."

The salary of teachers of aided schools is as low as Rs 3000 – Rs 5000 for three years, after which the teachers are made permanent.

Undergraduate with diploma	Rs 3000
Graduate with a B.Ed.	Rs 4000
Post graduate with B.Ed.	Rs 5000

In many schools the teachers are not only paid badly but are also herded like sheep without any consideration for their dignity or their individuality.

I recorded my anguish on this issue in an article which was published in the DNA Navi Mumbai on September 11, 2011.

"Are teachers paid enough?
By Vimala Nandakumar

India is supposed to be a developing economy. In fact, we have no money to pay the developers of human resource, the teachers, in the country. One example to prove my point: Junior college lecturers—post graduates living in a city like Mumbai are offered a salary of Rs 5000 a month! They will continue to earn Rs. 5000 a month for three years after which if they are lucky they may get their regular salary. Meanwhile they are expected to teach a class of 120 students, correct answer scripts of all the classes they teach and deliver quality teaching. In case they leave the college to join another, the three year rule will be applied all over again. In a city like Mumbai how does one live with a meagre amount of Rs. 5000, feed the family, educate children and live in decent accommodation? What is the rationale behind giving teachers a salary of Rs. 5000 a month? Domestic helps, autorikshaw drivers, nannies and chauffeurs earn much more than teachers . . . .

Teachers' Day is celebrated with great enthusiasm every year but the society is yet to give the due respect to the profession. Movies which highlight the poor status of teachers like "Do Duni Char" win awards at functions, but fail to impress parents and students. The movie was about a mathematics school teacher who comes under societal pressure to buy a car. He borrows a car to declare it as his own only to land into trouble with the car.

Ironically when a school organized showing this film for the students, the students came out of the movie hall, teasing teachers for their inability to own expensive cars."

Even after I worked as a temporary teacher in a couple of institutions I was undecided about sticking to the teaching profession. I had to rethink when some years later, young boys and girls greeted me in public places and introduced themselves to me as my former students. One of them is practising acupressure, another, a chartered accountant and the third a real estate agent. An interesting incident took place which decided my destiny.

One evening I was returning home after dusk in an autorickshaw. When I reached home, the driver refused to take money from me saying, "I won't take money from my teacher!" It is this incident which made me realize that the teachers' profession had not lost its sheen.

I decided to pursue the profession and to do B.Ed.

CHAPTER 3

TEACHERS' TRAINING

Wedded to the Bachelor's degree of Education

A bility to teach and having an interest in teaching alone would not be enough for one to be employed as a teacher. In addition to these, one should acquire the appropriate qualification so that one can be a good professional teacher. The B.Ed. course is essential for this purpose. It gives a teacher a sense of direction and offers a preview of the functioning of schools. The subjects taught in a B.Ed. course include psychology, school management and the philosophies of educationists. These subjects offer an aspiring teacher the much needed understanding of education.

Just as engineering students take up projects, doctors serve as house surgeons and CAs do an apprenticeship, teachers also go through practice teaching lessons and in-service training at schools during the B.Ed. course. Their assignments and teaching lessons are evaluated. So much is packed into a year's course that it is indeed a thin spread. Students of B.Ed. tend to wait for the course to get over. Many teacher trainees do not take B. Ed seriously. *This is the reason why teaching lacks quality in schools.*

Recently, in a campus interview to recruit teachers for our school 90% applicants for teacher's posts were rejected by our language consultant as their written English was pathetic. This reflects the poor quality of teachers who "pass" the B.Ed. examination. To add to the woes of schools, some B.Ed. colleges conduct education fairs where schools desiring to recruit teachers are required to pay an entry fee! A school which does not pay the entry fee may miss out on a good teacher. Only a few of the B.Ed. colleges maintain good standards. The others maintain standards that are below par.

The B.Ed. syllabus has not been updated for many years. Though the B.Ed. syllabus was updated in 2008 the changes were insignificant. This is ridiculous as the scenario in schools has changed dramatically over the years. *The curriculum for B.Ed. and Curriculum for the schools should go hand in hand to help teachers in teaching students effectively.* The B.Ed. curriculum should be dynamic.

The newspaper, DNA, reported on April 1, 2011 a proposal of the education department to overhaul the syllabus for B.Ed. The changes would require the teacher to complete her/his graduation and the B.Ed. course even for primary schools. Teachers would be given comprehensive training. For the first time, teachers would be trained in handling difficult parents. For example, the recently introduced "no fail" policy up to Standard VIII has placed the parents in a position to question the school if their wards are declared failed.

Copying teachers

The reason for the poor quality of trained teachers is not far to seek. I recall what happened when I was doing B.Ed. Some of the trainee teachers in the class were intelligent and hard working. They made clear class notes. Their journals and answer sheets were of such good quality that the professors thought it fit to compliment these trainee teachers. There were many predators among the other trainee teachers who would unabashedly photocopy the notes, journals and answer sheets of the bright students and submit them as their own without doing any work.

An incident was narrated by a participant in a teachers' meet. Once whilst preparing for a test some trainee teachers skipped the chapters on the philosophers because their professor informed her students that no questions on these chapters would appear in the B.Ed. exam! If the examiner chose to ignore the philosophers' views for the test, is this the way to "prepare" teachers for the profession? Even more basically, skipping this important portion in the examination can hardly be justified.

The trainee teachers had no compunctions about bringing answers scribbled on papers and even on their sari *pallu* and copying during examinations! Because of the lack of interest of the trainees in the teaching profession and their unwillingness to do hard work prompted one of the professors to admonish them. She said, "If you, as teachers, indulge in such malpractices, how will you instil values in your students? You should be honest to yourselves and quit doing B.Ed. as you are unfit for the teaching profession".

None of them thought it fit to quit B.Ed. Some of them must be heading schools now. One wonders how malpractices, among students and teachers, are being managed by them in their schools. Except for those who are genuinely interested in teaching, the teaching profession has come to be viewed as a career option by those who find themselves unfit for other professions.

A report by Manash Pratim Gohain published in the Times of India on January 2, 2013 was shocking. An excerpt of the report under the heading: "*99% fail test for school teachers*" is given here.

The results of the Central Teacher Eligibility Tests (CTET) conducted by the Central Board of Secondary Education (CBSE), declared on 27 December, 2012, showed that less than 1% of the 7.95 lakh candidates who appeared for the examination passed.

The CTET comprises two papers. Paper I is for aspirants wishing to teach classes 1-5 and Paper II for classes 6-8. Clearing CTET is essential to teach in any central government school. Delhi government uses CTET for recruitment of teachers for govt-run and aided schools.

In the CTET conducted in 2012, of the 2.71 lakh candidates who appeared for Paper I of CTET, only 2,481 passed. Of the 5.24 lakh candidates who appeared for Paper II, only 2,368 passed.

In fact since the examination was introduced in 2011, the pass percentage has been declining. This situation is a "wake up call" for the quality of B.Ed. degree being awarded.

This being the real background it is not surprising that the trainee teachers would often get stumped by some students in schools during their training period.

Learning to teach

Sometimes the trainee teachers would get baffled by the students. Once a student of Standard V said, "Mango trees remain firm on the ground because of the weight of mangoes they bear!" This remark was treated as a joke and passed off. It is left to the perseverance of the teacher to explain the role of the roots in the stability of trees.

A trainee teacher explained the first aid for snake bites. She taught them how tying a knot near the place where a snake bit would avoid the spreading of poison.

A student promptly asked, "If a snake bit a person on the face should we tie the knot around the neck?" The teacher was thrown off guard. A teacher should expect such questions and be prepared accordingly.

This is an example of how under-preparation on the part of the teacher can lead to the surrender of the teacher before the students in the class.

With the advent of internet the students are well informed and the teachers remain far behind. Today's children are digital natives and we, teachers, are digital immigrants. That sums up the gap between students' and teachers' understanding of electronic gadgets and being net—savvy. Many companies and private organisations are targeting schools to provide technology based lessons, lesson plans and assessments. Students in high profile schools bring lap tops or iPads to the classes. Some elite schools provide LCD projectors in every class rooms. It is left to the provider of these facilities to train the teachers. How many B.Ed. colleges have undertaken to make their teachers techno savvy? The schools and B.Ed. colleges do not keep pace with the current developments but function in isolation.

Now let us see the ***positives of the B.Ed. course***. The course is intended to make a teacher complete. This is how:

- The concept of lesson plan ensures that every aspect of teaching / learning is covered.
- The micro-teaching seminars stress on voice modulation, clarity of thought and language.
- Practice teachings in schools and the innovations brought in by the trainee teachers into lessons make children enjoy the class.
- An ideal lesson plan of a unit in a subject involved the following stages:
  - Introduction that is based on a current topic or something that interests the students and related to the lesson to arouse their curiosity.
  - Reviewing the basic knowledge of the students related to the topic.

31

- ○ Eliciting answers from the students by asking probing questions on the topic making them think in the process.
- ○ Making sure that the explanation is interspersed with new concepts.
- ○ Summarising the unit at the end explaining concepts which are new to the students.
- ○ A five minute question – answer session with higher order thinking questions for those students who are generally ahead of the class.
- • There were clear thought processes on making of the Time Table. For example, there are special restrictions about not having Maths in the first and the last periods of the day. The reason is that the children would miss out on the lesson if they are late to school and switch off mentally as he/she has to go home immediately after the last period. It is also recommended that Maths classes should be neither just before nor immediately after lunch breaks.

The B.Ed. course trains the teacher to be entirely student–centric. Some of the methods taught in the B.Ed. course may be idealistic but not difficult to practise. After passing the ideal B.Ed. course, once a teacher joins a "real" school the focus shifts from teaching students to "practical considerations". Most of the teachers unlearn what they were taught in the B.Ed. course. There is a huge gap between theory and practice which reduces the B.Ed. course to a mere formality.

Despite what they learnt in the B.Ed. course many teachers provide a lot of explanations in the class without giving credit to the students' ability to understand. Here are two instances of teachers' undermining the capacity of students.

Once, a teacher was explaining subtraction of numbers to the students of standard III. The class was in progress when one student got up to asked, "Can we subtract a bigger number from a smaller number?"

The teacher was taken aback because she did not expect this question. Before she could think of the answer another student in the class answered the question saying, "Of course you can but the answer will be negative".

How wonderful that was! The teacher should have jumped with joy and celebrated the occasion and made the boy proud for going beyond text book or the class. But none of this happened as the teacher was overwhelmed by her unpreparedness. She failed to applaud the child for his smart thinking. That is a sad reflection of how children are herded without regard for their abilities.

In another case, a new computer teacher during a demo lesson for Standard I wrote "Computers" on the board and asked the children, "Do you know anything about computers?"

Initially the children sat tongue-tied probably because they had been instructed to behave well in front of the new teacher. Slowly each one of them started answering, unable to contain the excitement the chapter created in them.

One said, "We see them in shops".

Another said, "My father works with a computer at home".

The third one answered saying, "My mother maintains an account of daily expenditure on our home computer".

One student said "I could see my little brother in my mom's tummy at the hospital computer".

The last remark stumped the teacher completely. She never turned up after the demo class!

Plain explanatory teaching is bound to be boring, unproductive and least stimulating thereby breeding indiscipline in the class. The emphasis of B.Ed. course on education being student-centric is often thrown to the winds. The trainees are taught to take teaching seriously so that the students find the lesson interesting. However, during the B.Ed. course, we felt discouraged to see some of our class-mates not taking the training seriously. At the same time, some of us felt encouraged when our practice teaching sessions which were considered to be model lessons were video-taped for future use. Elaborate arrangements were made by the teacher training college to record these model lessons.

Some of the experiments which I was encouraged to do in the B.Ed. course came in handy in my teaching career. For example, I was asked to teach a model lesson for Standard VIII on "Heart". I started the lesson with a slide of Laurel and Hardy and asked the students, "Which of the two was more likely to get a heart attack?" Hardy –was their obvious choice.

The introduction made sure that all the students got "hooked" to the lesson. Then immediately I started teaching them about the heart and its functioning. This was followed by a slide show on the functions of the parts of the heart. The slide show was accompanied by the heart itself speaking about its functions! For this purpose, the voice of a young boy was recorded and played during the slide show. In those days when there was no LCD projection, it helped in holding the attention of all the students. Certain lessons warrant a lot of efforts on the part of the teacher.

While explaining the characteristics of images in plane mirrors it was a challenge to get the students of standard VIII to understand lateral inversion correctly. I showed them a placard reading the laterally inverted version of AMBULANCE thus bringing the relation between real-life situations into the classroom. In order to bring excitement into learning I asked students to write a story so that it could be read holding a mirror. Students had fun writing the story from right to left and that too with laterally inverted letters.

As a trainee teacher when I went to a school to teach a class I found the students of the class a bit restless. I was to teach the unit on "Snakes".

I commenced the class with the picture of a snake charmer put up on the board and asked the students, "What was missing in the picture?"

They said, "Snake!"

The link to the lesson was established and caught their attention. Students who were exposed to such interesting teaching methods often requested these teacher trainees to come for longer durations of teaching. They were bored with their own teachers' "chalk and talk" methods. These teachers would have given interesting lessons when they did their B.Ed. but lost interest in teaching after joining schools.

True satisfaction in teaching consists in witnessing the sparkle in the eyes of the students that signifies that they have understood what the teacher just explained. A good teacher would go to great lengths to derive that satisfaction.

Now-a-days some schools do make a lot of fuss about being student-friendly. One example is an International School that I visited, where the Principal was making a time table for each and every student to suit his/her requirement. This was possible because of the low student to teacher ratio and the hefty fees which only expats and the elite of Indian populace could afford.

If the State provides the necessary resources to increase the number of teachers, then all schools can become more student-friendly.

CHAPTER 4

TO BE OR NOT TO BE . . .
TEACHERS IN A DILEMMA

Survival in schools

After acquiring the B.Ed. degree a teacher gets totally exposed to different environment in schools. All the theory about education being student-centric is thrown to the winds and she learns to handle lessons on survival in schools. Survival is not easy as the teacher often encounters difficult situations. The teacher has to weigh the correct options against the easy way out.

The two options of a teacher

Every teacher in his/her career is often faced with two options rather like "to be or not to be". Nowadays with the line between right and wrong or ethical and unethical getting blurred a teacher is caught between two choices. One choice would help her do her job, draw her salary and move with the flow. The other would invoke professional ethics and would more often than not interfere with her career prospects. Many teachers would go in for the safe and soft option. If a teacher on the contrary prefers the professionally correct option, she would be at the receiving end of the butt and ridicule of her "wiser" colleagues.

Invigilation versus relaxation

Malpractice during exams is an old evil practice. Some students would resort to bringing notes written in handkerchiefs or thin scrolls of paper and keeping them in the folded palms. (Notes would be written in such small letters that it would have taken a few hours for them to write extensive notes. It would have been better for them if they had spent the same number of hours in studying for the test). Probably no one in their homes was educated or interested enough. There are students who would resort to more intelligent ways of copying. They did all this right under the nose of an invigilating teacher.

In a school, some teachers had the bad habit of sitting during invigilation and reading magazines or novels. A student would get up from his seat to collect supplement sheets from the teachers' table. On the way back he would gesture to his classmates asking them to reveal the answers so that he could compare them with the answers that he had got.

During invigilation, a diligent teacher would be constantly looking for students who cheated during exams. When such a teacher entered the examination hall to invigilate, it was always interesting to see the reaction of the students. Invariably one or two would remark,"*arrey margaya re*". Very often such a teacher would catch the students holding slips of papers, handkerchiefs and written materials. Far from appreciating her for being vigilant, the other teachers would falsely claim, "The very sight of me would frighten the students so much that they would dare not copy. You are a novice and so students misbehave in your presence". They would completely distract every one's attention from the fact that it was *they* who turned a blind eye on the malpractices among students. Worse, they subjected the sincere teachers to unjustified ridicule. Students, even those who indulged in malpractices, knew the truth!

It would take much strength of character on the part of a teacher to overcome the dilemma as to whether to go with the flow or do the right thing and face the ridicule.

Innovating versus dull teaching

In some schools, a teacher who introduces innovations for the sake of the students is disliked by his/her colleagues. The reason may be either the colleagues' suspicion that the innovations are introduced to gain popularity or simple professional jealousy!

Co-curricular activities

I was overjoyed with the students of a school where I worked because they displayed creativity and extraordinary passion for learning. Even as they walked to the school the conversation of the students would relate to chemical bonding or some physics theory. But then, co-curricular activities were never a part of the school. I introduced some competitions like dumb charade, personality contests, Mad –Ad shows and Pictionary to the students of higher classes. The events were a great hit among the students. Students came out with more and more new ideas that took the school by storm.

Maths Club

In a school there were two types of students; namely those who had a passion for mathematics and those who dreaded the subject. I wanted to bring them together so that everyone would find mathematics enjoyable and entertaining. Therefore, I established a Maths club with the help of some enthusiastic students. It was conducted entirely by the students of standard XI every year for several successful years. The students would meet after the school hours and plan out games and *activities based on mathematics.*

Before the Maths club was introduced the students would sometimes skip the last period and trot back home but with the advent of the Maths club they willingly stayed back after school hours. Nearly 100 students joined the club. They split themselves into groups which bore names like alpha, beta, gamma and delta. Each group would conduct a competition for the other groups. The entire club activities were planned and conducted by the students. At the end of the year they would make a report on what they did during the year.

No recognition of this innovation came officially.

No contributions were collected from the students or from the school.

It was an entirely voluntary after-school activity.

We enjoyed the excitement that the Maths club brought us. Every year the Standard XI would take charge of the club, assume the same names of groups started by their predecessors and involve themselves in the club activities. The most interesting feature of the club was that even those students who were weak in maths enjoyed the activities. One of the batches brought out a magazine on mathematics. A

Maths Club website was created by the students. That was the time when computers had just started invading offices and homes.

Many years after leaving the school, one of the pioneers of the Maths Club wrote a letter from the US: some of her comments addressed to the members of the Maths Club, were as follows:

> *"I remember very clearly how my maths teacher asked us one fine morning if we were interested. We were altogether a very restless class and ready for some excitement. A Maths Club seemed like a great idea—a right mixture of maths and fun. It is really nice to know that the future batches seem to share that idea. I guess we owe a lot to our maths teacher and our Principal—without their enthusiasm and help, none of this could have happened . . . .*
>
> *You can't imagine the excitement when I went through the website. Even the group names seem to have remained the same . . . .*

In every academic year a "maths week" was celebrated by the Maths club. Typically, the events would comprise:

- Lectures on
  - interdependence of biology and mathematics,
  - interdependence of physics and mathematics and
  - Combinatorics and arrangements.
- Quarter hour talk: Lectures by students on topics in maths for 15 minutes. (A student spoke on the

digital root of a number which was a topic new to the teachers themselves!)

- Debate on "Maths is the most hated subject <u>because</u> of the maths teachers"

- "Wise guys show"—a maths event by ex-members of the club (A maze was given to the students and the ex-members would ask the groups questions in maths. If the group answered correctly, one wrong direction in the maze would be eliminated. This would continue until the groups reached the centre of the maze). Some questions that were posed:

  ○ Said one drunkard, "I spent one-fifth of my money and then one-fourth of the remaining and yet I spent $ 36.00". Was the initial amount divisible by six?

  ○ After giving Pascal's triangle as a hint, the students were asked to give the value of $^6C_4 + {}^5C_3 + {}^4C_3 + {}^3C_0$

  ○ What is the last digit of 7^{499}?

  ○ If the cube of a number + its square is twice the number then can the number be a natural number?

Such gems were presented by the seniors to those students who otherwise never thought maths was exciting. Every bit was done by time-consuming research and driven by enthusiasm of the highest order. *There was no internet at that time.*

- A lecture by an expert mathematician covering common mistakes in maths committed by students, division by zero, factors and divisors, importance of language in maths, precision, accuracy and exactness, indeterminate form, etc.

- Micro seminar –students picked chits on which certain topics in mathematics were written and spoke about them for 3 minutes (This meant that students had to talk extempore).
- Making models of "soma cubes" and "Mathematical maze".

The calibre of the students could be gauged from the fact that during a maths exhibition, the students spoke about topics generally taught at M.Sc. or M.Phil. level. A university professor who was invited as the judge was simply floored by the brilliance of the students that he adjudged two students as the best students for their extraordinary understanding of difficult topics (Godel's Incompleteness Theorem and Pigeonhole Principle).

The Principal of the school encouraged the Maths club activities. An exclusive room was allotted for Maths club activities. The room gave some space for the students to assemble and work on maths activities (This was too good to be true in a place where few teachers came up with innovations for the benefit of students).

A reporter of the Times of India interviewed the members of the club and published an article in the Times of India about this activity.

Excerpts from the article published in the Education Times, a supplement to the Times of India are given below.

The self-proclaimed mathophobic reporter noted that maths bug had bitten the eleventh graders and that the enthusiasm might be infectious. There was a bunch of Standard XI students who voluntarily stayed back after school hours to solve maths problems without any bribe of marks or being let off from sack-load of studies. Maths was something that most students either shunned or thought of as some drab and boring part of the curriculum. Through the maths club, they were trying to prove that the stuff in the text book was not all that maths is about.

The tradition of maths club had been handed down from one generation of eleventh graders to the next. Strategically placed between the horrendous burden of studying for the tenth board exams and the upcoming twelfth, the club was enlivening of the entire process of learning.

After basking in the glory of the newspaper report on the Maths club, strangely, the school authorities came down heavily upon this activity.

Finally, the Maths club was shut down with a bang on the face of the students!

Students can be encouraged to develop an aptitude for a subject through innovations in teaching methods. Maths club did exactly that. Here was a school which initially accommodated, later interfered with and finally closed the activity conducted by an enthusiastic teacher!

The dilemma for a teacher is whether to innovate and invite trouble or to stick to dull teaching.

Teaching versus coaching

Those days students got admission to a reputed coaching class in the city on the basis of the high marks obtained by them in the tenth standard. The coaching class had earned a reputation for making bright students shine brighter. The tutors there assumed that students had previous knowledge of many topics and rushed ahead leaving some students behind. The students who were left behind had to struggle to keep pace with the others. In our school, these students would request a teacher to conduct a bridge course for the coaching classes. This had to be done before the school started in the morning as the students had to rush to the coaching classes immediately after school hours. Thus the time for the extra classes was fixed as 7:00 AM. No member of the support staff was willing to report for work and open the class rooms at 7.00 AM. The only option for the teacher and these students was to sit in the open from 7 to 7.45 AM for the bridge course. They did this even in the cold winter mornings of December. This teacher was voluntarily filling the gap between the school and the coaching classes. The students benefited. That was her REAL reward!

Some talented teachers quit teaching in schools and opt for coaching students at home which is much less stressful and more satisfying. These teachers are not guilty of unethical practice.

Many teachers thrive on conducting coaching classes at home while working as teachers in schools. This is unethical. Teachers who conduct coaching classes can be distracted from their professional responsibilities. After all it is highly attractive to teach a handful of interested, bright students at home and collect tuition fees. In the school they have to teach a heterogeneous group of students including some uninterested ones in a crowded class room.

The loyalty of students and parents gets divided between school and coaching classes thereby creating an unhealthy school life for the students. Some schools have managed to dissuade their teachers from giving tuitions to the students. This is indeed laudable.

The dilemma that a school teacher faces is whether to conduct profitable coaching classes for her students while working in a school or teach well in the school so that the students of her class do not need any extra help.

Favouritism versus objectivity

School policies should apply equally to all students and not be allowed to change to suit every teacher's ward. Many teachers can be seen observing the school policies only as long as the policies suit them and their wards studying in the same school.

Teachers rally around their colleagues when it comes to internal assessment of exams of their wards. By mutual arrangement, teachers' wards are given full marks, irrespective of whether the student deserves the marks or not. In such situations, teachers' children have an edge over the other students whose parents are not working in the school. The result is an unpleasant atmosphere in the school spoiling the relationship between teachers.

The bright students who might happen to be teachers' wards would find themselves in the focus of unsavoury remarks about their genuinely good performance. Some collateral damage that!

Slackness versus professionalism

In some schools teachers enjoy certain privileges. Many teachers who live just a few minutes away from the school would report for work late. Some teachers living in far off places would come half an hour before time and if they occasionally reported late, they would be taken to task. The habitual late-comers would always sign the "right" time to escape being noticed whereas those who honestly signed the actual time of entry were open to criticism. The signal sent by the concerned authorities in such schools is that honesty is not a good policy.

One hears about teachers who walk into the school much after the bell rings at the beginning of the day and go home even before the end of the last period. They do not wait even a minute after the school hours. Such teachers have nothing to do with the school or the students except between the bells. Some teachers influence the preparation of the time table to make sure that they have no school duty in the first and the last periods. They could thus "look after" their home-front without the school interfering with their personal programme.

There are teachers and teachers. Some would stretch themselves to the limit to teach well. Their students invariably do well in the examinations. There are teachers who wash off their hands if their students fail. They never feel accountable. They would deny credit to the good teachers if their students did very well with the explanation that the students were bright and fared well on their own. Their message to the serious-minded teachers is this: "Do not try to do a great job of teaching. You had better be with us". The sincere ones are alienated by this attitude of such teachers.

There are some happy-go-lucky teachers who are honest enough to admit that they have taken the teaching job in the school because they are bored at home! Imagine the kind of damage their attitude would have caused to students of several batches!

Such teachers sometimes demand that they be given subjects and classes that suit their likes and dislikes. The school which obliges and panders to the whims of such teachers evidently is not student-centric.

Where do children figure in the scheme of things of such schools?

There are many instances of unprofessional practices among teachers. Let us see some examples.

The reader would have come across instances of teachers attending to their personal work during school hours. This way they would have their leave entitlement untouched for use at the end of the calendar year. The school would be without many teachers during the year-end. Students would enjoy because they got plenty of "free periods".

While some teachers skipped classes doing their personal things some other teachers would make a mental note of such happenings in case they needed ammunition for future use.

Teachers should maintain log books, carry out correction of notebooks in a timely fashion and respect the deadlines fixed for completing portions but many teachers default on these counts. The deadline given for correction of test papers is usually one month. On most occasions, the students would forget all about the test by the time they were handed over the corrected answer sheets. There was a case of a teacher who took 3 months for teaching one chapter and wrapped up 3 chapters in one month.

Under these circumstances the few conscientious teachers' promptness in correcting the papers would go unnoticed by the authorities but appreciated by the students and ridiculed by the colleagues.

If the management asks for innovations, prohibits the teachers from running coaching classes, demands strict adherence to the code of conduct for teachers and directs the teachers to write exams to see if they had adequate knowledge of the subjects they were teaching the consequences would be deleterious. Teachers who are used to flouting rules would find all that inconvenient. Anti-management and in effect, anti-school activities would intensify.

Do these teachers feel they are on the horns of a dilemma between professionalism and slackness?

Joining the Anti-Management Group versus remaining independent

In some schools nepotism, politics and favouritism rule and ruin the school governance. Rules are amended to suit some teachers. Such actions would invariably lead to the formation of an Anti-Management Group. Some of the teachers who want to go with the flow and would join the Group. The members of the Group would pose pertinent questions to the management. If they are not entirely satisfied by the answers provided by the management they may get aggressive. They may resort to strikes. They may force teachers to go on mass casual leave and boycott the school events.

In all this no one would be concerned about the students.

*Students are what a school is **ALL** about.*

The leaders of the Group would ignore the norms and rules laid down by the school in general. They would enjoy concessions and stay out of school ignoring their classes in the name of representing the teachers' woes to the management. The Principals would probably be caught between this Group and the management. The few *teachers who did not join the Group* would come to the rescue of the Principal by conducting examinations on schedule and holding cultural events even during agitations.

School work is time-bound. It involves the future of students. Disruptive activities by the teachers interfere with school work that will affect the students directly. In the event of a teachers' strike, how can the teachers face the students? The students of senior classes are bold enough to turn around ask, "What moral right do the teachers have to penalise the students for not attending classes when the teachers themselves stay away from classes?"

Does that mean that the genuine grievances of teachers should remain without redress? No. The concerned authorities should ensure that all outstanding issues of teachers are quickly and adequately addressed. If the teachers keep the students in focus they would put forward their grievances before the management without affecting the school activities.

The management should also be equally responsible and appreciate that redressing the grievances of the teachers in time has a direct bearing on the school activities. *A situation where one can arm-twist the other should be avoided for the benefit of the students.*

Teachers admit their wards in the school where they work for the sake of convenience. School fees would be low, if not waived for a teacher's ward. Their vacations would coincide. If the teacher whose ward studies in the school happens to be a member of the Anti-Management Group then the ward can expect favours to come her/his way.

Teachers who do not join the Group would be isolated by the members of the Group. The leaders of the Group would unleash verbal attacks on these teachers for not *being with them!* Even their wards can get victimised.

Whether the ward of a teacher is favoured or victimised it is unfair on the psyche of the child.

Isolation of a conscientious teacher by the colleagues is not rare and it can be very painful in addition to being unjust. No teacher would speak to the isolated one. The animosity would grow in intensity every day. Even if the teacher does or says the right thing he/she would be slighted. Under these conditions, a teacher is at the cross roads where she has to decide whether to join the Group and meet only those

CHAPTER 5
NO DILEMMA

In the face of a conflict

The conflict between the teachers and the Anti-Management Group is largely responsible for the dilemma faced by a teacher who wants to adhere to the professional ethics. It must be admitted that just as the teacher is justified in feeling strongly about her professional obligations, the Group is justified in working for the welfare of the teachers of the school.

The Anti-Management Group can argue that the benefits of their agitation accrue to the teachers who are not members of the Group as well and therefore these teachers should toe their line. The teachers who stay away from the Group can argue that adhering to their professional obligations is paramount to them and that not only the benefits from their agitations but even the blanket penal actions imposed by the management can reach the teachers who are not members of the Group. This argument for and against can go on *ad nauseum*. Therefore, each party should respect the principles of the other and not interfere with their activities.

Fair treatment to students

In schools some classes would always be more difficult to handle than the others. In one such class, the students were very difficult to handle as they had a sound knowledge of the subject. They were self—motivated and brilliant. Some teachers would prefer not going to those classes as they would get ragged by the students if their lectures were not up to the mark! Initially, at the beginning of my career, I was given all those classes. I faced a set back at the hands of those students but slowly over the years I worked hard towards handling them and my subject well in the classes. A teacher under these conditions is faced with the dilemma of avoiding such classes or preparing well to engage the students. I had no dilemma. I opted to engage the students.

Teachers should treat all students in an even-handed manner. This is particularly important in the context of determining the promotion results. A meeting was held for finalizing the promotion list of Standard IX. I was the class teacher of one of the sections of Standard IX. Two students had failed miserably – one was the ward of a school staff. It was suggested that the ward of the staff member be "promoted" but not the other student. Everybody seemed to agree with the proposal so as not to get into any controversy but I demanded the rationale for the different treatments being meted out to students in the same situation. I said, "Every student cannot have her/his parent working in the school. We should be fair to both the students and treat them alike." My colleagues were taken aback by my approach. Obviously no one wanted to support me though everyone agreed with my philosophy privately.

I learnt later that both students were detained in the same class! I would have been happier if both the students had been promoted. It was then that I understood that even if it is a solo voice of protest, demanding justice, it would be heard.

I did not blindly go with the majority. I stood for fairness and equal treatment to both the students. I had no dilemma.

Fair treatment to teachers

A teacher who questions the school authorities or her colleagues when their actions go counter to the interest of the students becomes a *persona non grata*. Hostility on the part of teachers towards her can take an ugly turn. If the isolated teacher, in addition, is not a member of the Anti-Management Group and performs her assigned duties against the diktat of the Group she may face more problems. The hostile teachers would target the students of the class of the isolated teacher to "teach her a lesson". Her students would be pulled up for no fault of theirs and treated by the members of the Group as the whipping boys so that she felt bad. That would be terribly unfair!

In an instance such an isolated teacher offered to resign so that her students would be spared of harassment in the hands of her colleagues. Ironically, some of the hostile colleagues pleaded with her not to leave the school in the middle of the academic year. The reason was not that they were very fond of this teacher and therefore did not want her to leave but that their wards who were studying in the crucial Standard X were in her class. Was that an indirect compliment? They would not mind if the teacher had resigned after their wards graduated from the school. They were not concerned if the other students lost a good teacher.

They did not care for the other students at all.

Under these circumstances, should a teacher continue in the job or resign to spare the students and herself from harassment? She would have no dilemma. She would resign from the school!

CHAPTER 6

TEACHERS – JACKS OF ALL TRADES AND MASTERS OF MANY

Jacks and masters

Teachers not only have to teach but they have to do a lot more. In some schools they have to keep account of students' school fees, organise field trips, correct board exam papers and much more. Apart from work related to the academic duties, teachers working in government schools have more tasks assigned to them. Teachers are no doubt jacks of all trades but they are also masters of many.

Multi-tasking jugglers

In addition to the multi-tasking within the school, teachers have to make all arrangements for school picnic including visiting the transport operators' office to organize the bus facility and negotiate for a concessional charge. This work is in addition to the many arrangements teachers have to make before, during and after school picnics. The responsibilities that teachers take during school picnics and field trips are too many and too obvious to warrant enumeration. Teachers working in a government institution are assigned election duty as well. School work takes a back seat when it comes to election duty.

Not only the teachers but the students are also impacted when teachers are sent to do election duty and census work.

Polls apart

Some years ago, soon after one mammoth election was over there was another when a party withdrew support to the government within a few days of forming the government. Apart from the millions of rupees spent, this event brought great suffering to the teachers from government schools. This practice particularly affects the students studying in government schools while it mercifully spares those going to private schools as teachers of private schools are not assigned election duty. The important point here is that teachers should do only teaching.

Some of the polling booths where teachers have to do election duty as the Polling Officers are located in areas where autorickshaw drivers would refuse to go. There are no decent toilets or ventilated rooms. In the polling station, teachers from outside the city limits have to spend the night prior to the Election Day in the polling station itself. They have to carry food and water on the polling days. The representatives of various parties seated in the polling booth are looked after by their respective party leaders who provide them food and water at regular intervals. Though teachers do belong to government run schools neither the school nor the government looks after their basic needs. *Teachers constitute a weak class who get exploited by all sections of the society.*

Teachers run the risk of being arrested if they decline election duty. The few police constables at the polling booth would have hardly been able to protect the teachers in case of booth capturing or some untoward incident. Teachers are paid a paltry sum for the entire risky assignment thrust on them simply because they are teachers in government schools.

Election duty is indeed important. People are required to man the poll stations. However, when teachers stay away from schools during the training for poll duty the students miss a lot and the teachers get overburdened too. The same argument applies to census duty also. The differential treatment meted out to the students and teachers of government schools, in this context, often passes unnoticed.

To correct the correction work

Another main concern in the teacher's job relates to the centralised correction of papers of the Standards X and XII. Students spend precious years preparing for the board exams. The future of the students depends on the marks secured in the Board Exam. The callous way in which the corrections are done by some teachers is most disturbing. Teachers are expected to examine 500 papers in a very short period of time. The Board authorities should raise the necessary resources, employ more teachers for correction of papers and ensure that a decent job of correction of papers is done for the benefit of the students.

Correction and moderation of answer scripts should be done in quick succession if not simultaneously. Once, a moderator for Standard X board exams fell ill during the paper correction. I was asked to don the mantle of the moderator. Most of the teachers who had done the paper correction were from outstations. Some of them had done a shoddy job. They had not assessed some answers. They had already left the town so there was no way they could be asked to reassess the answer scripts. As a moderator nearly 2500 papers were personally scrutinised and corrections were incorporated by me. If the moderation was also done in a shoddy manner, many students would have got less marks and their future admissions would have been affected.

The higher authorities require the marking of answer papers to be completed within a very short period of time. Thus speed, and not thoroughness, in correction of answer scripts takes priority. Many answer sheets were bundled so badly that often the last page or the attached graph paper would be lost in transit.

In another incident the moderator egged on the teachers to correct more papers. The teachers are not machines. They are worried about travelling long distances to reach home in time. Many schools where corrections are undertaken do not have decent desks and toilets. To sit for 8 hours a day and correct 500 odd papers could lead to neck and back problems. For doing this strenuous work the teacher is paid a measly sum. Even that amount would arrive a few months later and that too in instalments.

Teachers are exploited and as a result they display callousness. *The system should guarantee that all students get the marks that they deserve.*

A report that appeared in The Mumbai Mirror dated August 20, 2011, is relevant here. According to the results announced by the Board, a student of standard XII had scored an average 51% in French. On re-evaluation of the paper her score became a bright 75%. The updated mark-sheet that followed revealed that she had scored an outstanding 95% in French. After the corrections her average marks went up to 87.5 from 80.5 where even half—a percent matters. She could not get the subjects of her choice and had to settle for her second option for no fault of hers. How could she have scored three different marks? Such is the quality of correction that goes on in the crucial exams.

The authorities conducting board examinations should get more teachers to mark answer sheets and pay them well. After that, erring teachers should be taken to task if they do a bad job of correcting papers. The teachers should be paid not purely on the basis of the number of papers but the quality of correction.

Every school—whether government or private—should send teachers for correction *in proportion to the number students they send for the Board Examinations*. This way correction will take minimal time and the quality will not suffer.

This could be a fitting reward to parents who make sacrifices to educate their children. Above all, students will be spared of the agony of losing marks which later gets translated into losing admission to good colleges and a career that they desire / deserve.

CHAPTER 7

STUDENTS OUT OF FOCUS

You are not being watched

*O*ften the focus of schools is not on students. The behaviour of students reflects the kind of attention that they receive. Some parents blindly support the children. Then students become arrogant, wild and develop a devil-may-care attitude. Students know that they can get away with murder as their parents (or the neighbourhood "aunty", if she happens to be their teacher) would support them. This kind of "blind" support from the parents and others will be counter-productive in the long run. Good behaviour can be ensured by keeping a watch on the child's activities.

Instilling values

Many schools attach more importance to marks than values. Here is an instance: A student from the last bench in a class stood up and said that he had a problem seeing the board and wished to occupy a seat in the front row. The teacher requested someone from the front row to swap places with the student. No one moved. Then one boy changed place with the student. The teacher quickly concluded that the boy who offered to exchange his seat was a new comer to the school.

The teacher was asked by her students as to how she could guess that the boy was not from their school. The teacher pointed out to them that unfortunately their school attached importance only to marks and not values.

One school had groomed a student to be a Good Samaritan and another school ignored instilling values in students and the students knew well what was right but came heavily under the influence of the overall insensitive culture of the school environment. For the parents of the students of that school excellent academic performance of their wards was the ultimate goal. Nothing else mattered.

The school's responsibilities are not limited to the academics but include the holistic development of the students. Unfortunately, teachers, the Principal and the Management often think of little more than getting better and better results in the examinations.

Clever students

The teachers should fully focus on the students' needs when they are teaching, assigning homework and conducting tests. Otherwise they would be found out by clever students. In one of the schools where I taught there were many students whose parents were well educated. The ambition of these students was to go abroad by excelling in studies. They did extremely well in their studies, especially in science. The students were focused on academics more than their teachers were on many occasions.

In one instance, the students were asked in a mathematics examination paper to prove that the value of a determinant was equal to zero. The question was wrong as the value turned out to be 1. The students did not waste time asking for clarifications. They calculated the value as one and left the examination hall without further ado. They knew that the teacher was wrong. There were many such instances. The teacher would realize the error only after students in the examination hall pointed it out. This happened because the teachers never solved the question paper on their own before subjecting the students to the examinations.

In another case, a new teacher was asked to set a Physics question paper. She referred to a guide which provided the answer to the problem within brackets. She had copied the problem from the guide verbatim including the answer! Students had a blast that day. They came out of the hall confidently expecting full marks for that particular question. The teacher was not reprimanded or taken to task. The reason is that the head of the department had not checked the question paper before it went for printing.

That was the extent of lack of focus among the teachers and the interest they had in the students.

Trouble over students

The students whose parents were not well educated had another kind of problem.

Some of the students of a school were not groomed well at home and the school was apathetic towards them. They failed in most of the subjects and created nuisance to the school authorities and their school mates. Sadly the Principal and the teachers never took indiscipline as a challenge and ignored many instances of indiscipline. Some teachers learnt to control them by motivating them. Some teachers who could not tolerate their misbehaviour were constantly having trouble with these students. Some teachers invited the disapproval of the students. The harassed teachers would never share their experience with the colleagues because they knew that their incompetence would be exposed.

New teachers often felt that they were simply thrown to the wolves. They had to either swim or sink. Some teachers who were genuinely interested in the teaching profession learnt to swim against all odds. Those who could not went through depression as they suffered at the hands of unruly students. No help came from the management or the Principal. These teachers found solace in loneliness and were the subject of gossip by the other teachers who should have come forward to help their colleagues who could not "swim".

In effect, the incompetent teachers *could not* do much for the students. The competent ones *did not* help their counterparts. In such an environment what focus could have been turned on the students who lacked support from home?

The problem is not with the children

If the school had its focus on student welfare many problems would not have arisen. A few case studies would demonstrate the peculiar problems posed by students.

In a disturbing incident a student was involved in an altercation with a stranger in his neighbourhood. This stranger brought his pet dog into the classroom during the break time and set the dog on the student with whom he had the quarrel. The student was bleeding and said bravely he would manage the situation all by himself. He did not want any help from the school staff. The complete apathy of the staff, lack of security arrangements in the school and the authorities' studied ignorance of such incidents would shock any one.

There was another incident that took place during a farewell party for the senior students. This time the daughter of one of the trustees disrupted the programme. The girl claimed that no one could punish her as her father was an influential person. The other students tried their best to bring this matter to the Principal's notice but to no avail. They were discouraged by some teachers. It was a signal to the student community that knowing a person holding an influential position was a licence to misbehave. The Principal missed a golden opportunity to use his legitimate authority to instil some value in a misguided youngster.

Sometimes the focus of the school is confined to the wards of the teachers, Principal and Directors as observed earlier.

Even if the teacher's child is in the primary level he/she sees it as an advantage to be a teacher's ward. She /He would try to break rules and ask for concessions (e.g. coming late to school and non-submission of home work). The parent cum teacher would protect the child thereby sending wrong signals to the child. This pattern of behaviour would lead to formation of groups in the class and generally the teacher's wards would bully not only their class mates but also the other teachers! The teachers would support the wards of their colleagues or of the Principal so as not to get into the bad books of their masters.

In a certain school everyone was expected to accord special treatment to the Principal's ward. The Principal himself would conduct workshops on how children of teachers should be treated on par with the other students. He would, unabashedly grant special concessions to his own ward. If there were extra classes for students the Principal's son would abstain as he would have extended his holidays or for some such reason. He would go off for breaks without permission or informing the concerned teacher.

Any offence committed by the son of the Principal was pardoned. This was an unwritten law. No one agreed with this practice but no one would express it for fear of inviting the wrath of the Principal. The other students who indulged in such activities were discriminated against and penalised. The classmates of the Principal's son felt that they were given step-motherly treatment. The Principal's son was not to be blamed at all. It is the Principal who should have known the adverse effect that the special treatment would have on the personality of his ward. Such double standards set by heads create an unhealthy atmosphere in the school.

It would be in the interest of the ward of the Principal to study in some other school though it may be inconvenient in many ways. The ward would be able to lead a normal student life and also the Principal would be able to function effectively as the leader.

In a school the Principal introduced new criteria for creating different sections. She divided the classes into sections on the basis of the marks obtained by the students in the final exams of their previous class. She did this with the aim of getting better results. In all this the effect that such division would have on the students' psyche was completely disregarded.

The class teacher of the "best class" was asked to get best results from the students. The class was indeed terrific to teach but teachers handling that section had to be well-prepared and alert. The children were self motivated and had the ambition to get good grades. There were some students of this section who felt they belonged to an exclusive group and refused to mingle with other students. It is not that everyone in the section felt this way. There was a girl who felt miserable because while she was selected to be in the "best class" her best friends were left behind.

The creation of the above "best class" was based on faulty premises because the evaluation of the answer scripts of the previous year's final examinations was not standardised. The question papers were common to all classes. The students of the teachers who set the question paper had an edge over the other students and therefore they had performed better than the other students in the final examinations of the previous year. Some of the students who scored high marks did not really deserve to be in the "best class". Obviously some deserving students were left out of the "best class".

Let us look at the class which was branded as the "worst class". The teachers either constantly reprimanded them for poor performance or taught in a way that went far above their heads. "Sixer, sixer" or "bouncer" is what the students would call such a lecture. The teachers complained that they felt depressed teaching them as the students could not understand a word of what was being taught in the class. The class had a very low self-esteem and it required great efforts from all the teachers. I did not give up on my class of "slow learners". As their class teacher I encouraged them to take their studies seriously. *They had never been treated well nor motivated to do better*. It was an unwritten law that the students of the "worst class" deserved little or no attention. In fact, the students of the "best class" needed little attention as they were clever any way.

The "special focus" on some students threw ALL the other students out of focus. Creating distinction of any sort among students is always counterproductive in the long term.

My colleagues would have laughed at me if I had said that these students were bright but that only the system did not help them in securing good marks by throwing them out of focus. I was proved right to my joy.

Years later I walked into an investment firm where I found one of the students of the "worst class" welcoming me with a smile. He recognised me as I did him. For nearly five years thereafter he was "my investment advisor". He knew exactly when and where my investment would get me maximum return. I blindly followed his advice.

After all I believed in his abilities even when he was studying in standard X . . .

CHAPTER 8
STUDENTS IN FOCUS

Students' response to school's efforts

There are some schools that care for students. Students respond beautifully when they know that the school's focus is on them. A lot depends on the head of the school. The school contributes to the character-building of children to a great extent as children spend a significant fraction of their wakeful hours in the school. The behaviour of the children can be honed in the school through productive interaction with the parents.

Care for the students

I walked into a school not knowing that they were desperately looking for a maths teacher. I offered to teach mathematics in the school. Having taught XI and XII Standards, teaching IX and X standards was easy for me. The Principal was a dynamic person who became my role model. I worked part time and enjoyed every minute of it. Students were bright, good in sports and well groomed rather than being restricted to academics and lacking in other skills.

A "Maths Hub" was established in this school with the help of the students who had enthusiastically conducted the Maths Club in the school where I worked earlier. The students, the current and ex-students enjoyed the maths activity which was based on SAT and GRE. This was a novel experience for the students.

We had tried out "housie" in maths where the senior students generated problems with answers ranging from 1 to 99. The housie cards were then distributed to the junior students. The juniors would then solve problems and tick the answer on their housie cards.

Fun activities in maths called "Asterix vs Superman" and treasure hunt for "the trapped Princess" were organised for maths enthusiasts. The treasure hunt was based on decoding maths problem to find a place where the next clue was hidden. A lovely story was woven around the abduction of the daughter of a Tsar. The "abductor" challenges the people to find her and promises gift to them. Elves (Standard IV students) escorted the students of different groups to places which had the clues that would lead them to the next place. Finally students had to find the right key to the princess' cell.

The students will never ever forget the excitement that they had that day.

Students would stay back after school, devise new maths games and try them out on their colleagues. The school buses would wait for them while the students enjoyed the maths activities. The Maths hub helped in realizing the aim of maths teaching in schools, namely, to develop the right attitude and aptitude for the most dreaded subject. Somehow the majority of the teachers never agreed that maths teaching could go beyond solving problems. They only knew that practicing hundreds of problems would help the students get good marks in the board exams. No one thought *enjoying* maths was possible in schools. These students were the only ones to have included mathematics as an aspect of their alumni meets.

Some comments made by them about the Maths Hub are given below:

> *"All these years Maths was just a boring set of numbers, but now I find it really exciting. I never thought Maths could be so interesting."*— *Standard X student.*

> *"It is the greatest thing that happened since we joined school"-Head boy*

> *"The best aspect of Maths Hub, according to me, is that the students are allowed to organize various games and quizzes without the assistance of a teacher. We were given freedom to do so."*— *Standard X student.*

The school was fine in all respects. Children were fantastic. Of course when they reached the Std X the pressure of being in the class caught on and it became dull teaching the children who already knew the portions. They had no extra time for anything except running to coaching classes which killed the enjoyment of learning mathematics.

In the same school a Dutch student and I were given two groups of students who were subjected to yoga and aerobics. The foreigner was to study the effect of yoga on emotional reactions to maths problems of students. It was an interesting research programme. The school participated in such interesting research activities because the students were always in the focus.

These activities build a strong bond between the teachers and the students. The students were good not only in academics but also in sports and in soft skills. One ex-student of the school plans to help his father in his business and another, a girl, has become a pilot.

Kudos to the Principal of that school for keeping the students in focus and encouraging innovations for the benefit of the students! The students deserve all credit for responding beautifully.

Children's Character

Character building is as important an aspect of schooling as it is of parenting. Many students display graces. Many students lack graces because of the shortcomings of parenting and/or schooling. The above-mentioned student who plans to help his father in the business was the head boy in his final year of school. He broke his leg during the sports day in the month of December and was in crutches for nearly two months till the board exams. Not once did the parents come complaining to the Principal to blame the school for the mishap. On the last day at school, the boy gave his farewell speech sitting on the ground with his bandaged leg stretched.

In another instance, the results of a board examination shocked the teachers and the Principal alike because one of the students who normally fared exceedingly well got much lower marks than expected in one of the subjects pushing him to the fourth position in the school. His paper was sent for revaluation to the board. We knew that the actual marks would arrive late. At a function organised for the merit holders, medals were given to the first three in the board results. The third position in the merit list went to the head boy.

Many months later the actual marks after revaluation arrived. By that time the students had left the school and joined colleges. As expected, the updated third rank went to the student who had been pushed to the fourth position in the school ranking. Nothing could be done by the school. To our surprise and delight the head boy who was earlier awarded the prize for third position came to the school to return the medal. *He graciously said that he did not deserve it and that it must be rightfully given to his classmate and dearest friend.* These days when students resort to unethical practices to achieve their goal, here was a boy who was sure of what was just and fair. *Of course, the medal, the Principal said belonged only to him.*

Shocking behaviour

Students often surprised me with their conduct but a couple of them shocked me with their behaviour.

We used to notice a boy who was very aggressive since the day he was promoted to the international section from the local education board. The teachers and the coordinators of the primary local board had been postponing addressing the issue, probably in order to appease the parents and not upset the management. We did not have a regular counsellor visiting the school thereby leaving the counselling to be done by the teachers!

During the school film shows this boy would turn his face away from the screen if the film wasn't the one of his favourites (e.g., Mr. Beans.) Anyone who dared to oppose him in the class had to face his tantrums. His class mates understood his moods and always supported him.

Once he was asked in the school to make a card on the occasion of Mother's day. He actually drew a dagger with blood and a wounded lady as his mother.

It was grisly.

We spoke to his mother. We came to know that the boy protested in this manner against his mother's second marriage. This incident demonstrates how much responsibility has to be taken by the school and the Principal.

In another incident a boy of Standard VIII was missing from school for many days. When we called his residence no one answered the calls. No one had a clue as to where the boy had vanished. The teachers naturally got anxious to know the whereabouts of the boy. They consulted the administrator before bringing it to my notice. I sent a fax his father stating that his name would be struck off the rolls if he did not report to the school immediately and regularly. My intention was to caution the parents rather than harm the future of the child. He was as precious to me as the rest were.

The next day the boy sneaked into the class room to attend school. Obviously the classmates of this boy had warned him about the possible serious consequences and hence he had come to school. After probing the matter we came to know to our horror that every day the boy would leave the house dressed in school uniform and with some pocket money accompanied by the driver, visit a cyber cafe to spend the day there and return home after the school hours. The parents were under the impression that the boy was attending the school regularly. But for my persistent efforts the boy would never have been rescued from this situation. Heaven knows what kind of company he was keeping!

Focus! Focus!! Focus!!!

Students are simply adorable.

I have always exhorted the teachers in the schools where I was the Principal to keep the students in the focus. Students' welfare includes all aspects of schooling such as academics, sports, behaviour, character, personality, punctuality, hygiene, nutrition and co-curricular activities. Students' welfare should be the main focus of a school.

CHAPTER 9

LACK OF INFRASTRUCTURE IN SCHOOLS

Get set go!

A new teaching institution should first establish the necessary infrastructure before it starts functioning. Some institutions are established without the basic infrastructure. Consequently, one sees so many ad hoc arrangements in such schools which defy established rules and often even logic! The consequences of severe shortcomings can be harmful to the cause of education. It is the responsibility of the every staff member and the Principal to identify the corrections that need to be made. The management should correct the situation without delay.

No desks for students!

A newly established school recruited staff after the due process. Most of the students were from local "displaced families" and hence admission for them was assured. The school faced many teething troubles such as class space, furniture and funds. One wondered why the managing trustees wanted to start a school without even the basic infrastructure. There were only desks for 65 students in a class of 75. The Vice-Principal once commented, "Let us *hope* there would always be 10 absentees every day". This was indicative of the attitude of the top officials of the school.

Unhygienic toilets

The toilet is the most neglected area in any place in our country, be it home, office, train, public places or school. I noticed immediately after taking over as the Principal of a school that toilets were not cleaned by the support staff regularly. To make matters worse, students would throw trash into the closets. The support staff would complain that they had to remove the trash which they resented, obviously. The staircase, school corridors and the playground were littered with bottles, cartons, chocolate wrappers, etc. I was surprised that this littering did not seem to bother anyone.

Every one complained but no one took action. I issued strict instructions prohibiting the students from throwing trash all over. Immediately the littering stopped. The toilets were not clogged any longer. I appealed to the students to maintain cleanliness as they themselves were responsible for the school being clean. I sensitised them to the trouble the support staff faced in maintaining cleanliness in the school. I went on regular rounds. Students understood the seriousness of the issue. Improvement in cleanliness was evident. Sometimes the results are not seen instantly. One needs to be perseverant. Hats off to schools which give importance to this aspect!

In a school the open house provides an opportunity to parents to register complaints such as the lack of clean toilets. Preschoolers would not realize the effect that unclean environment could have on their health. But the older children would know. Once parents complained to me that their children suffered infections because of the unhygienic conditions in the school. I could not possibly ignore the complaints though I was instructed to do so because "parents always complain!" An extra rest room was created for preschoolers at my insistence thanks to the support from the management.

In another instance, a sixth grader refused to use the dirty toilets and her parents were pained by the psychological effect it had on the child. I called the girl alone to my office and assured her that she could use the restroom attached to my office in case she wished. The parents were happy that I listened to their concerns. This could not have been a long term solution. Many schools are not too worried about this basic need of students. Students spend nearly 7 – 8 hrs in the school. A hygienic environment should be assured to the students. There should be no scope for compromise in this matter.

Recently government seems to have taken the issue of lack of toilets and drinking water seriously. Here is an excerpt from an article from The Hindu (dated 3 October 2012).

The Supreme Court had directed all States and Union Territories to ensure that basic toilet facilities, in particular to girl students, are provided in all schools within six months. A Bench of the Supreme Court had issued its direction on a petition from the Environmental and Consumer Protection Foundation since it was informed that the court's direction issued in October 2011 was yet to be implemented by many States, which sought further time.

The court had observed that right to free and compulsory education of children in the age group of six to 14 is part of the fundamental rights guaranteed under Article 21-A of the Constitution of India. This right could not be enjoyed unless basic infrastructure is provided by the state. Parents were reluctant to send their children, particularly girls, to schools where basic toilet facilities were not available. The direct consequence would be breach of children's fundamental rights guaranteed under Article 21-A. The court had directed earlier therefore that if it was not possible to provide permanent toilets, then at least temporary toilets should be provided on or before November 30, 2011 and permanent toilets be made available by December 31, 2011.

The Chief Secretaries of all States were directed to ensure that separate permanent toilets for boys and girls were constructed in all schools on or before March 31, 2012.

Technology in classrooms!

Modern technology that invaded your drawing room and kitchen has entered the class room and why not? It has come late! It is heart-warming that modern technology provides teaching aids. Teachers are inadequately trained to handle these gadgets. Often there is mismatch between the contents of these teaching aids and the curriculum followed by the school. There are frequent power failures. Uninterrupted Power Supply systems are expensive. Time is wasted in procuring and maintaining these gadgets. A software expert who is supposed to be available in-house often remains inconspicuous. The teachers have a tough time driving a motor car and a bullock cart all at once. Much time is wasted in blame games between teachers and the management. The newspaper DNA dated 2 Dec 2012 carried an article "Tablet based class rooms". The government has promised the Akaash 2 to students, but the teachers are yet to be trained. Research into digital learning has just about started. Will Akaash 2 become yet another unused gadget in schools?

Some educationists feel that government should deal with issues relating to digital pedagogy first. Successful education initiative is not hardware-specific. There are no answers to questions like what are the effective ways of using tablets? What part of the syllabus goes into the tablets? What are the ways of using tablets?

Bill gates in an interview said "You really have to change the curriculum and the teacher . . . . The device is not the key limiting factor at this point."

According to Arundati Chavan the president of the PTA United forum, Mumbai, "Teachers need to be motivated and trained to prepare study material and lesson plans using technology. In our experience, teachers don't want to do extra work."

With enough time and effort, teachers can be convinced to incorporate technology in their lessons. The Digital Equalizer Programme, run by the American India Foundation, conducts a training programme for teachers to integrate technology and teaching in public schools. The duration of the training programme is three years and classes are held once a week. "I don't believe in intensive training where teachers are trained for 15 days and then left alone. You need to follow up with them to ensure that the training is applied," says J Sundarakrishnan, Director, Digital Equalizer Programme. It takes nearly a year to build rapport with teachers and convince them that new technology can be useful, says Sundarakrishnan. They are then given smaller goals that are achievable. "The idea is to empower teachers so that they can be the judge of how computers can be used to explain concepts to children."

Absence of Playgrounds

Playgrounds are essential for each school. In metros where space is a premium, many schools function without, or on borrowed, ground space. This limits the outdoor activities of students. Outdoor activities are an important aspect of education but often not recognized as such. Because of this, sports and sports teachers receive less respect than they deserve. Students are forced to play in corridors and class rooms causing nuisance to other classes. Such restricted indoor activities are unhealthy for the students.

When the students' energy for playing is not properly diverted, indiscipline breeds in schools.

School bus and children's safety

The interfacing between the school authorities and the transport operators should be smoothened to assure children's safety. Some schools provide transport facilities to students and teachers. Some school managements believe that provision of facilities for operations outside the school campus is not their responsibility. Much can be said for and against the positions taken by schools. Responsibilities in this regard should be accepted and implemented by the concerned parties. That would be in the interest of the students.

Not a drop to drink

Availability of drinking water is vital for children. In many schools pure drinking water is not provided. The water tanks are not cleaned frequently. Water purifying gadgets are not installed. If the supply of water brought from home gets exhausted, children would have no option but to consume water which may not be suitable for drinking with predictable health hazards.

Comprehensive external auditing of school infrastructure should be undertaken more effectively and regularly.

The student community is putting up with the defective infrastructure offered by schools innocently, trustingly and silently.

Is this how we look after the future of our country?

CHAPTER 10
A STUDY IN PERSPECTIVE

How schools function in other countries

This chapter is included with the intention of providing a better perspective about the schools in India. I got an opportunity to work in a school in Indonesia. The setting of the school was overseas but the institution was managed by Indians settled in Indonesia. I am presenting this chapter in two major parts, viz., my experience as a teacher and the turn around that one could bring about even as a debutant Principal. The management and its overall caring attitude deserve a mention before I discuss my experience as a teacher and a Principal.

A management that cares

The members of the management of a school in Indonesia interviewed me for the post of a Mathematics Teacher. The interview was held at the Taj Hotel in Mumbai. Instead of dilly-dallying, immediately following the interview, they expressed their willingness to employ me. Accordingly I signed a contract for two years. The tickets, the letter for obtaining visa and the rules and regulations of the school were provided to me. I was informed that apart from free accommodation (with free electricity and water) and transport, the school would give us a month's salary as bonus and three major vacations—for Ramzan, Christmas and summer. This assurance was duly fulfilled!

When we reached Jakarta we noted that the accommodation for almost all the teachers was ready. The teachers were taken straight from the airport to their respective apartments. The air conditioned apartments were fully furnished. Grocery supplies for a whole week as well as fresh food for the first day were kept ready. During the bus-ride from the airport to our apartments each of us was given 500,000 Rupiahs which we thought was a huge amount of money. Little did we realize that the price of everything would be in multiples of 1000 rupiah (about Rs 6=1000 rupiahs at that time). The cost of bread was 6000 rupiahs, while it was available for Rs 12 in India and that of a small lunch packet 18000 rupiahs. We were taken to a Wartel (i.e. a PCO) to make phone calls to relatives in India. The first call that we made was paid for by the school. One or two of us had no ready accommodation and hence were accommodated in a hotel near the school. These arrangements made by the school management left a good impression in us. All this showed us that the school looked after its teachers well.

This was a new experience for us.

In addition to all the facilities, the management offered free **International Baccalaureate Diploma Programme (IBDP)** for two children of their teachers in their school. In India the fee for this programme is very high. If the teacher had to educate two children for IBDP he would have had to shell out money equivalent to his annual income. The teacher and children would arrive at the school every day with great enthusiasm. The teachers were happy to teach and gave of their best to the management that looked after them well.

The management scored on two counts, viz., that the teachers were extremely productive and teacher attrition was arrested.

No special treatment was expected to be accorded to the ward of a teacher in the school!

Experience as Teacher

The school building was huge and painted in white and royal blue. The upholstered chairs were also blue in colour. The exterior was tastefully done. The students were a mix of Indonesians, Chinese and Indians. The school campus was beautiful – what with spacious classes and a theatre with a capacity of 300. There was also a swimming pool. The frontage of the school had two basketball courts.

Some of the members of the management themselves were alumni of the school. The Principal and the teachers did not want to be harsh with the students. In any case the students had everything in life including expensive mobile phones and large amounts of pocket money. They knew that they had their family business to fall upon once they completed schooling. Some of them were not much interested in studies. At that time I noticed that some students found games and play stations more exciting than "O" or "A" levels of University of Cambridge.

On the first day of the school, every teacher came into the staff room narrating the lack of discipline among the students of their classes. We were used to some amount of discipline in schools in India and were unnerved on hearing the stories of indiscipline. The students laughed loudly and cracked jokes in Bahasa Indonesia, the national language of Indonesia, at the new teachers. The new teachers did not know how to react. The students' discipline always has a bearing on the teachers. The students were restless because often they had to go without teachers. Here is why:

When new teachers struggled with the issue of handling the students, some of the old teachers did not come forward to help them. Many teachers returned to India after the contract and a fresh lot replaced them. One teacher who came with us to Indonesia left the school without completing the contract. He was homesick and also probably was new to teaching subjects of international curriculum. He just could not adapt to the new place which was challenging both personally and professionally. He had left his family behind in India. As per the contract a penalty / compensation of $3500 should be paid if the teacher broke the contract.

One Good Samaritan among the teachers took charge of the situation and bailed out the teacher by offering to pay the compensation, a sum which was gracefully reduced by the management. I appreciated this gentleman who was my neighbour and asked him as to how he could take the risk of lending money to an acquaintance to which he replied "woh mera paise leke ja sakta hai, meri taqdeer thodi leke ja sakta hai?" (He can take away my money – not my destiny). Good people are everywhere, only we have to recognize them. I was informed a year later that he was repaid the amount by the teacher who left the school. That adds up to two good persons!

There was another teacher who came to Jakarta with his family. During the December holidays he and his family travelled with us but when we returned to Jakarta after the holidays we found them missing. We heard that the teacher had quit! We gathered that he had come on six months leave from a school in India where he was working, just to check if the new job suited him. Since he could not handle the new job he left without informing the school authorities!

There was another case of a teacher who left Jakarta using the return ticket given by the management at the time of appointment immediately after joining. Both these teachers escaped paying for breaching the contract, had a free trip to Jakarta and rejoined the same school where they worked in India. The management on their part took every effort to recruit qualified teachers before the academic term.

Such incidents forced students to go without teachers and miss classes. The persevering sincere teachers had to cover up for those teachers who deserted the school.

Many of us who faced the same challenges there decided to stay on and honour our commitment to the school. That was our strength. The students realized in due course that they could not misbehave with us as we were willing professionals.

Students cannot be forced against their wishes to take part in certain school activities. For example, activities such as literary clubs and mathematics club were introduced at the end of the day. These activities should not have been relegated to the end of the day. Students who were not interested in these activities were free and had to stay in the school until the school hours were over. This resulted in a large number of restless uninterested students being left unsupervised while teachers were engaging some students in the various activities inside the classrooms.

Some of these uninterested students would sneak out of the school scaling the low compound walls and run away before school ended. The security personnel would go crazy trying to control these students. We had to install grills over the compound walls so that the students would not escape easily. I do not blame the students for all this. After all, schooling is all about helping the students realize their potential and channelize their creative energy. The management was ready to provide all support. It was for the Principal and staff to devise the methods to achieve the goals.

We decided not to give up disciplining the few errant students. We told the students in a firm tone that we meant business and would not tolerate indiscipline. We learnt the meaning of the words in Bahasa which were being hurled at us and readied ourselves to face the students with confidence. Fluency in English language was our strength. We engaged them with lessons which they could understand and relate to. Slowly students began to realize that we meant well by them and would not be scared away back to India. I saw an increase in the number of students opting for mathematics from 3 in the first year to 15 in the second and 40 in the third year.

We decided to remain strict with the students. I recall an incident when I asked the students sitting in the library to maintain silence. One of my students, Ashok, retorted in an impertinent manner encouraged by the presence of some big bullies. The next day during my class, I advised Ashok not to get carried away by the company of bullies and that he should behave decently wherever. This boy apparently had reported this matter to his bully friends.

The following day, I was teaching a class when I saw Anil, one of the bullies at the door. Anil stood there 6 ft tall gesturing me to come out.

I was under the impression that he was calling some friend of his and asked," Whom do you want?"

He said, "You Ma'm. I want you to come out."

I resented my class being disrupted. I quickly went out of the class room and asked him "What do you want?"

"Why did you admonish my friend, Ashok yesterday? What wrong did he do in the library?"

I told him "You know very well that you and your friends were making noise in the library and that was wrong".

He immediately demanded, "What proof do you have to say that we misbehaved?"

I replied calmly "I don't walk around in the school with a tape recorder or video camera. Ask yourself."

The student left muttering something to himself. I did not discuss this incident with any of my colleagues and went about doing my work.

The next day the Principal came rushing to the staff room. She settled on a seat and asked me if any student troubled me. I said that Anil had and I settled the issue then and there. She informed us that the management had come to enquire about the incident and wanted to call me to find out more details. Obviously the incident was reported to the Chairman by one of my students. The Chairman instructed the Principal not to tolerate such acts of indiscipline in the school.

I respect the members of the management for taking the correct stance.

In my heart of hearts I knew that Anil was not at fault. He was after all a young 16 year old misguided boy. If the Principal makes him a prefect and treats him like a hero for being a bully he will try to exercise his power. That is what he did. If you talk to such young bullies in a firm tone and tell them what is right and what is wrong, they would mend their ways. Children are the easiest to handle.

When I became the Principal I appointed the students who were role models to the rest of the students as prefects. Anil noted it and he changed dramatically and became friends with me. A year later, when he was studying in a university in Malaysia, he visited the school as an alumnus and was extremely polite and sweet.

A debutant Principal

As the time of completion of my contract approached I started getting ready to leave. The management came up with a surprise package. They requested me to become the Principal that too for the next two years. After giving some serious thought to the offer I accepted it but only for a year because of my personal commitments at home. I said I could come back after my husband retired and stay on as Principal as long as they wanted me to. They generously agreed. Without any delay they provided me with a chauffeur driven car, change of furniture and increased salary and bonus – even without my asking. I then put on the mantle of Principal of the school where I taught mathematics for the past two years.

The year I spent as debutant Principal of that school was career-wise the most memorable one for me. The management appointed me as Principal only because they had faith in me. Therefore, they did not constantly interfere in the school matters once I took over as the Principal. Many changes could be brought about in the school with the support of the management and the staff. Our focus remained entirely on the students and their welfare.

Student discipline

One of the first things that I did was to reconstitute the prefect body. Students who were good at academics, sports and above all exhibited exemplary behaviour were chosen to head the students' council. This set things right and students willingly followed the rules laid down by their own students' council. Their conduct improved dramatically. The canteen was kept clean. After the lunch break, students left for classes without any delay. Big dustbins were bought and placed in strategic locations. It ensured that littering stopped in class rooms.

Recognition to all students

The practice so far was that only the talented students were kept in the lime light. They grew in confidence while the remaining 80% of the students got ignored completely. I decided to make around 100 children come up on the stage for the good traits they displayed such as discipline, punctuality, and academic improvement to receive awards on the last day of school. It was celebrated as "Recognition Day". The parents of these children proudly attended the function. The students were selected after taking into account the teachers' feedback. It was kept a secret so that the students' excitement could be captured live and also that of their parents. It was such a delight to see the astonishment turning into smiles on the students' faces when their names were announced along with their exemplary traits which were recognized.

School assembly

The purpose of holding school assembly every day is that students should get together every day in the morning. A sense of belonging and unity among students develops during assemblies. Announcements made during assemblies reach the all the students of the school at one go. Students take pride in their contribution to the school during assemblies. Students are asked to come on stage for their significant achievements in academics, sports or any co-curricular events. These events motivate other students to do well in school. In short, assemblies are actually intended to provide an important platform for focusing on students.

During my predecessor's time, every morning, the whole assembly would wait for the Principal to arrive in the hall. She would invariably arrive late. After becoming Principal, I used to reach the school at 7 AM every day. I made sure that the school assembly started on time at 7.30 AM.

I made the students themselves conduct the assembly. Every class was given an opportunity for a week to conduct the school assembly in the morning. Each class was given time to come out with creative ideas of conducting the assembly. Points were awarded to classes for the innovations that they introduced in conducting the assembly. This resulted in a healthy competition among the students. An overenthusiastic class enacted a murder mystery serial on all the days of their allotted week which ended with the suspense filled climax on the last day. The students of the class were thrilled to see the audience applaud their efforts. In the earlier two years the assembly was a dull routine filled with rambling long speeches mostly by the former Principal, eating into the teaching time. The new format changed the assembly into an interesting daily affair which everyone looked forward to. It was always completed within the stipulated time.

Assemblies are of the students, for the students and by the students. This idea got firm reinforcement during my tenure.

Good practices

In order discourage late comers, the school gates were closed after 7.30 AM. The students' council was made in charge of checking, recording and reporting details of late comers. Students started arriving on time. Points were given to classes for cleanliness, punctuality, theme-based decoration of display of class boards and performances in academics and sports. Above all, students who showed exemplary conduct or registered improvement in academics were recognised. Some students who generally failed in a subject worked hard and showed improvements in the subject. They were recognised and rewarded on the Recognition day. Special kids who did not show great academic scores but had good conduct were given "The Principal's award". The class which scored maximum points was given a trophy for "The best class". The school changed for the better as students noticed that their contribution to the school was recognised. The erstwhile bullies started showing excellent behavioural changes so much so that it was difficult to differentiate the "good from the bad"! Students became the main focus for all right reasons.

Students can never be "bad" by themselves. Branding students as "dumb", "useless" and "notorious" still happens in the class rooms, corridors and definitely in the staff rooms. It is very common for the teachers to openly criticise or comment on students. As a Principal, during staff meetings I would request teachers many times never to indulge in this practice. I would suggest that only the concerned teachers should be informed about certain students' misconduct or misbehaviour and the discussion be kept confidential.

Co-curricular activities

I had learnt from my experience of the previous two years that students were in no mood for anything towards the end of the day as they would become restless and hyperactive. I wanted the school activities to bring some joy to the students.

Certain co-curricular activities were reintroduced for an hour but in the morning soon after the assembly every day. That one hour was given to the teachers to provide intense coaching to students who were preparing for the board examinations. Inter-section football and basketball tournaments took place during this hour. Practice sessions for functions, sports day or annual day took place simultaneously during this hour.

On certain days a few students would be free as they were not part of the activities in progress. Films like, "Jumanji" or "Home Alone" were shown to such students in the auditorium. Teachers had no issues of discipline as the students enjoyed themselves because extra classes, practices, sports and entertainment took place in an organised manner. The school functions were popular and so were the sports events. Teachers and students enjoyed every moment in the school as school activities interested them.

Tuition classes for weak students

The school permitted the teachers to conduct tuitions in the school campus after school hours for the students who desired extra coaching. A nominal fee was fixed for the teachers who took the extra effort. In order to make the coaching classes more effective, the number of students per batch was limited.

Even this coaching programme was not adequate for English. For the first time in the school the English Improvement Programme (EIP) was introduced. For a special batch of students who needed extra help in English, a pre-test was conducted. Intense English coaching was done for a long period of time. A post-test on these children registered improvement. What made these classes interesting was the fact that the students worked on puzzles and cross words instead of listening to lectures.

Special coaching for IGCSE and A levels

Saturdays were non-working days. Indonesians love weekends. The government would shift holidays that fell on any week day to either Fridays or Mondays so as to ensure that the whole country got long weekends to enjoy. Long weekends were welcome, but we needed to work harder with the students who were not ready for IGCSE or A levels. Special coaching classes for the IGCSE and A levels were introduced so that students could fare better in exams. The staff co-operated. The management did not interfere and thereby indirectly encouraged the Principal to do her best for the students. The classes conducted on Saturdays helped in the improvement of the results. The results of the IGCSE exams that year broke the records of the previous years.

Erratic Re-tests to organised tests for students

In the past there was a practice to allow students who missed class tests to appear for a retest. This was fair because if students were unwell, a chance was given to them to score in class tests. Some students misused this opportunity to a great extent. They would demand a retest if they missed it due to lack of preparation or if they had gone on a holiday or did not attend school for some reason. They would prefer a day convenient to them for the retest. They knew that the Principal would blindly support them. Sometimes teachers, not knowing how to handle the situation in the absence of support from the Principal, would be forced to conduct many retests and yet the students would fail in them. It burdened the teachers unnecessarily.

After I took over as Principal I changed the practice and conducted all the re-tests on a fixed day after the final day of the tests and ensured that all those who missed the earlier tests got one – just one—opportunity to write the tests. Thereafter the students did not come demanding a day convenient to them. This came as a big relief to the teachers as their work got organised better. Students realized that they could not fool around. They came prepared well for the tests and the genuine cases were given a chance to give re-tests immediately after the actual tests got over.

On the cultural front

Working in an Indian school in a foreign land calls for exercising sensitivity in one's actions and reactions. I decided to bring about the right perception to the students about the two countries to which they belonged! Indonesia was ruled by the Dutch. The Independence Day of Indonesia is celebrated on the 14th of August every year. It was decided to combine and celebrate the Independence days of India and Indonesia. Plays depicting some scenes from the pages of history of both the countries were enacted during the programme. The highlight of the programme was a play on the declaration of Independence of Indonesia. A student dressed as President Sukarno delivered a speech as the Indonesian flag fluttered followed by the melodious Indonesian National Anthem, "Raya".

Dandi march stirs up emotions in every Indian. We made students dress up in Gujarati attire as followers of Gandhiji. One of the students was dressed as Gandhiji. We enacted the Dandi march with Gandhiji preparing a fist full of salt on the stage with a rendition of Vaishnava janato in the background by a teacher. We had a song and dance sequence on "pagdi sambhal " –choreographed brilliantly by an Indonesian student who had never visited India. The dance had scenes of atrocities by British soldiers and conveyed to the audience the significance of Pagdi being a symbol of honour.

The cultural event ended with a fashion show on the traditional dresses of India with A.R.Rahman's Vande mataram music in the background. This programme was accompanied by a slide show that displayed regions of India and the Master of Ceremony brought out the essence of National Integration by a beautiful narration. An exhibition-cum-sale of pieces of art and craft made by teachers and the students was organized. The members of the management bought the craft and art materials just to encourage the teachers and students. The proceedings were donated to a school for slum children. The entire programme was acclaimed as the first of its kind in the school and was appreciated by one and all. The teachers and the students were given the entire credit for putting up on stage such a wonderful programme.

The cultural events that were organized by the school drew the attention of the national press. A report about the school entitled, ***Ethnic harmony flourishing at an Indian school,*** appeared in Jakarta Post, a popular daily, dated 23 March 2005.

A senior staff member of the school who taught Bahasa Indonesia was quoted as saying that the Indian and the Chinese students in the school not only co-existed peacefully but also integrated harmoniously with each other.

The report noted that the school promoted quality education. Though the school initially had a predominantly Indian student population, as the school's reputation grew through the years, the demographics shifted to its present balance, where two ethnic groups, the Indians and Chinese, were equally represented in the more than 1,200 students studying from kindergarten to high school. The school had the reputation of not witnessing the slightest hint of racial disharmony.

The report included the following lines about my views on the school:

> *The school's Principal, Vimala Nandakumar, said that she was proud of the school's diversity and harmony, which she attributed to the student's broad-mindedness.*

> *"Unlike adults, children see other kids, no matter what their background, as children," said Vimala, who was recruited from India three years ago.*

She said that she was surprised at how well the Indonesians of Indian descent had blended into society . . .

"If they were from India, they would be crazy about cricket," said Vimala, who has also been teaching mathematics for 22 years. ""My boys don't like cricket.""

However, she said that despite being Indonesian, "they know that some part of them is Indian and are very proud of their heritage"

Community service and Kartini schools

Community service should be integrated into the curriculum.

Indonesians largely believe in community service. A few schools for slum children were named after Kartini—a noble woman of Java province.

Raden Ajeng Kartini was born on 21 April 1879 in Jepara. She was a leading feminist. She worked for women's emancipation in Indonesia. Her father was an assistant for the district chief of the city. Her first dream was to become like her mother, working hard for others. She went to a Dutch school but when she was 12 years old her father prohibited her from continuing her studies because of the tradition—a noble girl was not allowed to have a higher education, they had to be secluded.

Ibu Kartini was very concerned about the education of Indonesian women. Because of her concerns, she founded a school only for women in Indonesia. Kartini always discussed feminist matters and revealed her dream of equality between men and women in Indonesia. She died at the age of 25.

April 21, is celebrated as *Ibu* Kartini Day in schools of Indonesia.

One of the "Kartini schools" was run by two Indonesian sisters. The schools run by these sisters were meant for children of labourers in the vicinity of the location of the school. The schools were constructed with four temporary walls with the fly-over serving as the ceiling. On the Gandhi Jayanti Day our school decided to adopt a Kartini School for a year.

The students of our school were already aware of the importance of social service and jumped with enthusiasm and ideas. They vied with each other to be part of the teaching team which would visit the Kartini School on Saturdays. Some taught English while others Mathematics. The most touching aspect of those classes was that there were mothers carrying small children in their hands peeping into the classrooms from outside. They were worse off than the ones inside such dilapidated schools.

The students organised a fair for the students of this school on Children's Day. The students put up stalls with games and food (prepared specially by their mothers). The students of the Kartini School in turn brought some handicraft items made by themselves to our school. The highlight of the programme was a film show of Bollywood dance sequences. The entire school staff danced on the stage with the students. The students of Kartini School were given gift hampers at the end of the programme. They were given lessons on computers assisted by student enthusiasts from our school. Uniforms were distributed at the end of the year from the donation that was made by the students.

The students of our school wrote an article on the adoption of the Kartini school. The article entitled, **Our favourite school,** was published in the "The Jakarta Post" dated 1 May, 2005. In the article they described how in keeping with Gandhi's tradition of charity, our school decided to 'adopt' a special school for children of poor garbage dump workers with the objective of providing further development. The school had around 45 students in their rolls.

During one of the daily assemblies, they were told of a project that was still in its early stages by "our thoughtful Principal Vimala Nandakumar" [I had told them that the school could not even afford electrical fans to cool the students while studying, never mind air-conditioners like the ones we had installed in our classrooms. I had described the school's dirty and unpleasant surroundings, and the lack of maintenance of the few classrooms they had. I had suggested that all students donate generously. Donations could be anything, ranging from unused school uniforms, books, food to stationery, and not limited to just money. The Community and Social Service Club was thus formed.].

In their article the students described in detail their visit to Kartini School along with me. They were shocked by its woeful condition. They could bring themselves to believe that children actually studied there only after seeing some children clad in tattered primary school uniforms and dirty casual outfits accompanied by some teachers emerged to greet them. What surprised them was the excitement reflected in the students' eyes; the children appeared to be immune to the desolate surrounding.

Our students then proceeded to teach them basic English words in one of the classrooms, such as words for parts of the face, names of various colours, numbers from 1-20, etc.

In their article our students observed that though it was a small classroom every child present in the school cramped in to listen. Some children could not get in, so they watched the class from outside and tried their best to follow what our students were teaching. After teaching, they played games by asking questions related to what they had just taught. Those who could answer correctly were presented gifts, either a snack bar or a pencil.

Our students remarked that these children learnt rapidly and most of them could answer very well. Their ability to learn matched their eagerness to learn new things. A student from Aceh (rehabilitated after Tsunami orphaned her) thrilled our students with her smart behaviour and diction. After the English lessons, it was time for story-telling.

One of our students read them a kindergarten storybook. The children were very silent as they listened attentively and excitedly. Our students, in this article admit that this good behaviour was something that rarely happened in the classes of schools that the more fortunate children went to!

Though most of the children were shy and did not utter a single word of thanks they smiled in gratitude.

Our students observed contemplatively in their article that they gained the same amount of benefit as these children did – their reward was the feeling of helping some people in need.

Our students had invited these children for a charity bazaar in our school. It was a very touching gesture that each child took our students' hands and kissed them, gratitude in their eyes and humility in their attitude.

The article was concluded with these words:

> *With hope in their sights, it is not hard to foresee a brighter future for Kartini School and its crop of not more than 50 students. But it isn't time yet to rest on our laurels; for what has been done for these needy children is only a drop in the ocean. As Robert Frost says: . . ." I have miles to go before I sleep."*

To make a difference to the teachers too

A Principal has responsibility not only to the students but to her staff as well. Over the two years when I was a teacher I saw what was happening to one of the staff members but as her colleague I could do mighty little. One of the teachers who had come from India with us was not very good at spoken English. She was eager to make friends with the rest of the teachers. All her efforts failed. The teachers' room was small and some teachers would pass snide remarks about her. She would be upset when students misbehaved. International curriculum was totally new to her and she could not grapple with the nuances of teaching. She would have done a good job if there was some help from the Principal or the other teachers.

All that she needed was a prop to make her realize her self-worth. When I became the Principal I gave her support in terms of encouragement and opportunities and was there a change! She blossomed into a different person. She came out of her shell and volunteered to help the other teachers in their tasks. She was assigned important responsibilities. This made her realize her self-worth. She was a good singer. This talent was used during school events. As the Principal I was glad that I could make a difference to her personality and career.

I made arrangements for teachers to attend seminars and workshops, increased their remuneration for correction of papers, provided transportation for teachers who stayed back for extra classes and organised picnics for the teachers.

Ever-supportive Management

The management of this school in Indonesia was different from the ones in India. The members of the management seldom interfered with the day-to-day working of the school and left it to the Principal to manage. All of them participated in all the functions organized by the school. Their cheerfulness and involvement always boosted our morale.

My debut as Principal was an exciting experience for me. It was apparent that the teachers and the students shared the excitement. Many of my former colleagues and students are still in touch with me. All good things have to come to an end. It was with a heavy heart that I bade goodbye to the wonderful school and the city of Jakarta.

Two years later, true to his word, the Chairman of the Jakarta school called me on one fine day and simply said "Vimalaji aap vapas aajayiye". Unfortunately at short notice I could not

CHAPTER 11

PRINCIPAL – THE PIVOT

Principal's independence

In any school the Principal, as the name implies, plays a pivotal role in conducting the school activities. She/He interacts with the management and implements their policy in running the school. She has to deal with the teachers, supervisors, non-teaching staff, students, parents and the individuals/organizations that have an interface with the school. She can be seen as being at the centre of all school-related activities. She is generally not entitled to the vacations enjoyed by the teachers and the students.

I know a Principal who was merely a person with a lot of responsibilities towards the school but no authority, contrary to the belief that a Principal was all-in-all in a school. In the name of feedback and reporting on the school performance the management constantly guided, monitored or advised her as to what she should (and should not) say or do in the school. There were occasions when she acted in the interest of the students but the management admonished her for not consulting them beforehand. As a result when she consulted the management on certain issues, they admonished her, this time for her "inability to act independently"! How can any Principal function in such a stifling atmosphere? The management should require her to seek their permission only in respect of certain pre-identified major issues. Within a defined framework the Principal should be allowed a certain amount of freedom. It would only increase the efficiency of the school administration.

Only in a few schools in India, Principals have a certain degree of independence in implementing the policies of the management. These schools have earned the reputation of being the best schools in the country. The Principals who do not have this independence have to follow instructions that come from the management, on a daily basis, in many cases. Otherwise, they would be transferred if the school had branches or their life would be made difficult.

The selection of a Principal

The selection and appointment of School Principals is a tough job for the management. Often an outsider is selected as the Principal. Sometimes a senior teacher from the same school would be appointed as the Principal. There are challenges in both cases. The outsider has to wait until she is "accepted" by the staff. Some of them might have expected to be anointed the Principal and therefore, disappointed over the selection of an outsider as the Principal. On the other hand, if one of the teachers of the same school is selected for the post, her colleagues, particularly the senior ones, would have resentment. After all, this teacher was sharing the staff room with all the teachers till the other day and now is at the helm of affairs supervising them! In one instance, I could sense this sentiment when the management of the school where I taught Mathematics appointed me as the Principal. Some teachers did not like the prospect of one of their peers—that's me, becoming the Principal. It was a reasonable sentiment.

A new school had advertised for a Principal and I was called for three rounds of interview. For the final round I was asked to give a presentation to share my vision of the school and describe where I would take the school in the next five years time. I was excited naturally because it would be great to work in a new school setting up systems and processes, creating a new culture and introducing innovations. I knew that it would be a a challenge. I decided to accept the offer. After all I was going to set a trend for the school as the Principal –with emphasis on hard work, professionalism, sincerity and excellence. The management went through a thorough selection process that reflected their seriousness about appointing a Principal who would implement their vision.

Challenges faced by a Principal

Many challenges are faced by a Principal in the schools in India. From the time of appointment as Principal, often the management, Directors and trustees treat the Principal as a mere intermediary between themselves and the school at large. They overlook the fact that a Principal is entrusted with social and legal responsibilities.

To undo and re-do

Schools which have had to do without a Principal for a while have a peculiar problem. The teachers and other staff get used to the idea of "working" without a leader. They become a boat without a rudder.

In one of the schools when I took over as the Principal my attention and energy were diverted to rectifying all the wrongs first. I found the staff room full of rubbish such as useless papers, charts and even used paper tea cups. I told the teachers that I would not have a staff meeting until the rubbish was cleared. The teachers most of whom were young had got used to the idea of idling at school and not treating the school as their own. It took me a couple of months to make them derive satisfaction from the work and develop a sense of belonging to the school and pride in their institution.

The teachers, until then were working with a coordinator who never came on time. There was no proper time table. Teachers were expected to go to any class that was without a teacher. Some teachers would never go to the class and the sincere teachers would find themselves taking impromptu classes for almost the entire day without a break. Undoing this culture was a major challenge faced by me as the Principal.

Often teachers, support staff and parents resist when discipline and order are insisted upon. Orderliness only brings better working conditions that reduce the stress on the students and teachers. The resistance vanished after the benefits of the changes intended for students became evident. Schedules were drawn up for teachers. Classes happened according to a time table. Teachers and students came on time. Parents, who till then were given a free hand, withdrew and the support staff realised that they could not fool around. The shirkers got noticed and were pulled up. Teachers could no longer take school work lightly. Faced with such challenges a Principal would need to function more like a strict police officer on duty than a Principal leading a group of dedicated teachers.

The Principal short-circuited

In some schools, the Principal has to report to a local centre of power appointed by the management as a kind of Chief Executive Officer (CEO). There could be nothing wrong in the appointment of a CEO to ensure that the Principal conducts the school in accordance with the philosophy of the management. The Principal would, however, feel cramped when the CEO dictates every minute action of the Principal and the teachers and when the CEO listens to "advice" which are sometimes gratuitous and sometimes sought by the CEO from her favourite staff. Such advice may be preferred over that offered by the Principal in her professional capacity. The Principal who has been selected and appointed after a lot of care and consideration on the basis of the judgement of the trustees may get sidelined by her staff and the CEO! In such situations the favourites would tell the CEO what the latter would like to hear rather than what would benefit the school in the long run. This happens when the CEO and the Principal operate in the same premises through the day.

The solution to this problem is that the CEO offers general and specific guidelines to the Principal and allows the latter to execute the instructions so the Principal may effectively function as the leader of her team.

Principal, the pillar of support

In one instance, some of the teacher-cum-bullies resisted the changes introduced by the new Principal as they found these changes "inconvenient". They thought of registering a complaint against the Principal with the trustees forcing the mild conscientious teachers to sign the memorandum. Faced with such pressure tactics, some Principals would appeal to these teachers to abandon the memorandum and promise to withdraw the inconvenient rules. This would set a wrong precedent and disillusion the conscientious teachers.

Once when I faced such a situation, I told the teachers that they were welcome to correspond with the trustees but only through proper channel. They noticed that I was not angry but was merely insisting on discipline in their protest. They decided not to submit the memorandum to the trustees. That sent a message to the trustees not to encourage teachers to communicate directly with them without the Principal's knowledge. This incident gave the sincere and conscientious teachers a big boost. They felt that their efforts would be recognised by their Head. The message was clearly conveyed that *we are all together here for the students of the school.*

Principal, the judge

Some teachers have the habit of physically harming students in the class. The students of lower classes are vulnerable. The little ones may not be in a position to offer any defence when teachers and others harm them. They may get intimidated by the teacher in the class. No one in the school has the right to touch any child. Parents entrust their wards with the school authorities believing that the school is a safe place. If teachers, the very people who are supposed to provide protection, hurt children for whatever reason, it amounts to breach of trust.

Some parents take it seriously and complain to the Principal against the teachers. They are justified in doing so. Some parents may have their own biases against some teachers! It is the responsibility of the Principal to assume the role of a judge – to be just and fair to the children as well as the teachers and not to be guided by the parents' bias, if any. After making a thorough enquiry into the matter and also speaking to the concerned teachers and students, warnings should be issued to the offending teachers, if they are guilty. In certain extreme cases, teachers may have to be directed to leave the school for not complying with the rules of the school, in the interest of the students.

It is a tragedy for both the school and the teacher to sever ties abruptly. The beleaguered teacher will have difficulty in getting another job and the students will be left without a teacher until another teacher is appointed. Extreme restraint and total control over one's temper will ensure that the teacher never finds herself in a tight corner.

Principal, the motivator

A teacher who does good work deserves to be recognized and appreciated by the Principal and the Management. It is an important motivation for the teacher to remain conscientious. Earlier in my career there was a Principal who recognized my efforts. In a Principal's conference, she presented a paper which was prepared based on my inputs on making mathematics exciting. She was gracious enough to acknowledge my contribution to the paper. When I became a Principal, I made it a point to appreciate the teachers just as my Principal in the past did.

In one of the schools it was a practice to applaud all those who contributed to events in the presence of the parents of students. Not only that, a letter of appreciation was given to those teachers. This created a happy environment in the school and the teachers remained motivated to do their best for their school. I further extended this initiative to the administrative staff and the support staff. They were thrilled because their efforts got appreciated too.

Principal on duty 24x7

A Principal who takes her profession seriously is on duty 24x7. This can be stressful and can interfere with her personal life but it is unavoidable. I had a testing personal experience when the teachers in our school did not come forward to accompany students on an outstation field trip.

During field trips students learn to travel and look after their own needs while away from home. After announcing a tour, the programme should not be cancelled except under extreme circumstances. The teachers should take interest and responsibility and actively participate in such tours.

Some students of our school registered themselves for a tour to a wildlife sanctuary during the holidays. The senior teachers for some personal reason refused to accompany the students. I, as the Principal, could not allow nearly 20 students to travel with just two escorts without any senior teacher though the parents of these children seemed prepared. All students were of age less than 13 and one was hardly 10 years old. The responsibility for the safety of young girls and boys weighed heavily upon me and I decided to escort them. Parents were overjoyed to see the Principal accompany their wards.

The place chosen by the tour operators offered good-accommodation, food and other facilities. There was a night trek into the jungle which looked more dangerous than adventurous to me. We walked through narrow paths, in the night, between thorny shrubs. It was our luck that we did not get bitten by snakes or some insects. The river crossing exercise was more dangerous than I imagined. I had my heart in my mouth when a girl student almost drowned in the gushing water due to her own weight before she came up above the water level.

I decided to call off the awful exercise and advised the adventure tourist operator to engage the students in less threatening activities. The students enjoyed the tour thoroughly.

I recall, however, that at the end of the tour came the shocking news that my mother was seriously ill. I could not abandon young students and therefore had to return to Mumbai with them. We reached Mumbai early in the morning and as soon as the students were safely handed over to the parents I boarded the flight to my native place to see my mother and be at her side during her last hours.

When can a Principal quit, if he/she wants to?

Once when the Principal of a school submitted her resignation, a trustee remarked that the timing of the resignation was wrong. It was the month of October. The Principal's job does not begin and end exactly with an academic year. The Principal is not entitled to summer holidays. In some schools, the Principal is not entitled to even one day of leave during the probation period of 6 months. It seemed unfair as the Principal was required to visit the school even on Sundays. How was she to function without a break?

Throughout the year the Principal is engaged in school-related work. October-November is the time when planning for the following year, recruitment, budgeting and admissions for pre-school start taking place. After that, the appraisals, training of teachers, induction of new staff, etc. commence. Then the process of preparation for the new academic year follows. In addition to teaching, the academic year is full of events such as open houses, field trips, celebration of national days, sports day, annual day, conferences and seminars. This is a continuous cycle and whenever a Principal leaves, the timing could be termed as inappropriate because many tasks are bound to be left incomplete. When is the right time for a Principal to quit if he/she wants to for whatever reason?

Principal and creative pursuits

Traditionally the Principal is feared because of the so called "powers" that she is perceived to possess. Teachers, students and even many parents would like to be in her good books. A Principal is indeed not merely the Captain of a team but a player in the team which has its task cut out. The members of her team should approach her without fear with any suggestions for the improvement of the school in all aspects. In addition to the above tasks, the Principal has to be an instrument of educational evolution in her own sphere. This has to be done through innovations. Such innovations need to be introduced by the Principal herself. Innovations forthcoming, if any, from the staff should be encouraged by the Principal!

CHAPTER 12

LITTLE INNOVATIONS BIG RESULTS

To encourage creativity

It is essential for the Principal to encourage innovative teachers and support them. In addition, the school and the students at large would benefit if the Principal herself innovates. This chapter which is essentially anecdotal based on my experience demonstrates the significance of introducing new interesting activities in the school which make learning an enjoyable experience and the school an attractive destination for staff and students. If a Principal is allowed to bring in improvements, the management should be given the due credit. Only with the cooperation of and support from the management it would be possible for the Principal to be effective.

Sports uniform

The sports uniform in many schools is generally white. Actually different shades of white are seen. In my school, in order to make it easier for the parents to maintain the uniform I suggested that the sports uniform be changed into colourful T-shirts and black trousers. Initially, the trustees did not approve the suggestion but later agreed.

They were convinced after the following benefits were pointed out to them:

a) The students of the school were too young to maintain the white uniform and it was particularly so in the case of children of working parents.

b) The T-shirts had the name of the "Houses" of the students. Students were seated according to their houses during inter-house competitions. Points were awarded to "Houses" for discipline. Points were awarded to the "Houses" for excellent behaviour and reduced for bad behaviour. It could now be ensured that competitions went off smoothly and without any hitch because the "House" could be easily identified from the name written on the T-shirts.

c) During field trips, judging the "Houses", in terms of behaviour of the students, littering, raising a racket and monitoring performance of tasks became easy because the "House" of the children could be identified through the uniform.

Because of the cooperation of the management, the benefits of the suggestion were enjoyed by all of us.

Litres and litres of litter

It is common that students litter wherever they are, be it the class room or a picnic spot. If some teachers merely lecture the students on a few occasions about cleanliness, no results would be seen. They have to lead by example.

I cannot forget the first field trip of the students of my school. We had packed food in aluminium foils and water in disposable sealed cups. We distributed the food in the bus itself so that they would not litter the place of visit. Even before we stepped out of the bus at the destination, foils and used cups were thrown out of the bus by the students. We had given them huge trash bags for collecting the foils and cups. Apparently the students were not instructed about collecting the trash. I pointed out their lack of civic sense to the students and made sure that the trash from the ground was picked and collected in the bags meant for it. Initially the students hesitated. I initiated the exercise by first picking up some foils myself. When they saw the Principal clearing the litter, they quickly followed suit. After this incident, the students stopped littering trash be it their class rooms or the places they visited during the field trips. Children are wonderful learners and take pride in sticking to rules, provided the leader sets an example.

The training the children receive in the schools will stay with them for life. Our cities and towns are so dirty with filth thrown around because this aspect is not taken care of in schools and organizations.

The DEAR Ones

In our school we introduced the Drop Everything And Read (DEAR) – programme: The habit of reading books is neither inculcated at home nor encouraged in schools these days. There are a few exceptions to this rule. The main reason for the poor performance of students in tests and exams is their limited vocabulary. Only reading habit can enhance the vocabulary of children. We decided to do something exciting for students to hook them on to book reading.

It worked.

Under the DEAR Programme, everyone in the school was informed in advance to bring a book with them to read. Each class had a mini library. Magazines in Marathi and Hindi were also purchased for the support staff. Ten minutes were randomly allocated to this reading session. We then selected three students who had extra energy and made one carry a placard saying "DEAR programme begins", the second one ring a bell and the third carry a bag full of books. These students would run in the corridors covering all the floors and also the ground floor where the office was situated. *As soon the bell was heard everyone in the school would drop whatever they were doing and start reading the book they had brought.* If they did not have one, our enthusiastic volunteer carrying a bagful of books will give them one to read. There used to be pin drop silence during the 10 minutes. Articles about this appeared in two or three newspapers.

We did not stop here.

Every month end, in the assembly two students, a boy and a girl, would be crowned "The Master Book worm" and "The Miss Bookworm". We would interview students and go through the list of books they read and ask them questions on the books, characters, etc. The standard of English did improve. Everyone in the school, students and staff alike got into the habit of reading. What they read during the ten minutes was the mere appetizer. Many of them pursued the reading after the school hours. There was an article about the DEAR Programme in the newspaper DNA dated 5 July 2007.

Junk in the lunch box

Many parents, merely to suit their convenience and save time in the mornings, pack junk food such as finger chips, fried stuff and such calorie rich snacks, in the children's lunch boxes. This in spite of the care that they professed for the health of the children! Our school appointed a nutritionist to monitor the nutrient value of the sumptuous snack provided by the school in addition to supervising the hygiene of the school kitchen.

Students quickly were weaned away from junk food as we decided to appoint a food-check squad comprising a few students and a teacher. The squad got busy peeping into the lunch boxes and awarded points to those who got healthy food to school. The odd one would be identified and was forced to abandon junk food.

A circular from the school on the choice of food that was easy to prepare and also nutritious was sent to parents. They whole heartedly supported the school. The classes started scoring better on this account as well.

Celebration of Father's Day and Mother's-Day

It is important to keep the parents informed about the happenings in the school. In fact, they should be encouraged to get involved in certain school activities. I would send circulars on topics relevant to parents periodically. I organized workshops for the parents and that proved useful. We celebrated "Mother's day", on a week day. Teachers organised interesting games for girl students-mother teams.

The surprise part of the show was inviting mothers of teachers to the school.

"Father's Day" was celebrated specifically on a Sunday to please the students who demanded that they should also get a chance to invite their fathers to school. I should and did appreciate my ever-willing staff for accepting the additional work on a Sunday. Students proudly brought their fathers to visit the school. The involvement of parents in the school celebrations brought about a good equation between them and the school.

The management deserves credit for allowing the Principal and the staff to organize these events.

The Sports Day

Any parent who sought admission for their ward in a school would first enquire if the school had a decent playground. Mumbai is a place where many schools are requesting the boards to relax the requirement for a playground as there is a space crunch. If there is space available, the price is sky-high (We are talking about grounds!). The Sports Day had to be conducted but our school did not have its own ground. We hired a nearby playground. The event was spread over two days.

In any sports event, it is a common occurrence for children to get injured. The school management ensured that two nurses and ambulances were stationed at the venue on both days. Students sang "To be number one" at the inauguration of the event. They had practised it every day in their classes while the song was played on the public address system. The craft teachers, assisted by the other teachers, made especially for the sports day, a huge dragon for the dragon dance. The Sports Day concluded with an event for the parents, in which they participated with enthusiasm. The preparations made for the Sports Day ensured full attendance on both days. It was a grand success. It set a tradition.

A feedback mail on the Sports day sent by the husband of a teacher was greatly appreciated by all.

Dear Vimala ma'am,

Thank you very much for inviting me at the Sports Day function. I never had an opportunity to be a part of such an impressive event during my school days.

I find talking about you, the school, teachers and events irresistible. The occasion was undoubtedly a grand success. You set such high standards for all while leading from the front. Full marks to you in the litmus test of leadership!!

In her welcome words to parents, a teacher appropriately mentioned that a school organises the Sports Day event for developing lot of traits among students including team spirit, fitness, building confidence, sportsmanship, cultivating the art of winning and accepting defeat and coordination.

T–together E–everyone A–achieves M–more.

Right from the march past, wonderful welcome song on freedom, speech by chief guests, dances on seasons, dragon dance, crazy cricket and various competitions, each event was an enjoyable experience and there was never a dull moment. Although I missed last two dances on seasons and majority of dragon dance, I enjoyed crazy cricket the most. Hats off to you and the teachers for inventing this hilarious concept and remarkable to see the children responding to it in their own thoughtful and creative way. Some of the expressions were just unforgettable. Certainly not criticising, but felt that the time interval between competitions was a bit long. However, that could not steal the honours of the day from all of you in anyway. All credit and compliments to you, the PT teacher and the team for their stupendous efforts. Truly believe that endeavours succeed or fail because of the people involved.

Must admit that I was amazed by your enthusiastic participation in the running race. A fantastic example of sportsmanship and inspiration to all out there.

Regards from an unofficial sports correspondent

Exciting events and performance peaks

The Taj Mahal Project

Students look forward to some excitement in school life. Once the school children took interest in the debate that was raging in the media on whether the Taj Mahal should be declared as one of the man-made Seven Wonders of the

World. Students participated with great interest. Many came up with strong arguments in favour of the Taj Mahal. Taking advantage of the topical interest, we organized a mathematics project for the seventh graders in which the students were asked to draw "Taj Mahal" on the floor and calculate the approximate area occupied by the picture. The students used the tiles on the floor in place of a graph sheet!

Adoption of a Municipal School

A municipal school in Mumbai required help in English and mathematics. On the 2nd of October, we adopted the school. Every Saturday teachers accompanied by some students would visit the school to teach the students English, Music, Maths and Craft. The students of the municipal school enjoyed doing worksheets distributed by the English and mathematics teachers. The craft teacher supplied material to the students who came out with extraordinary art and craft products.

Science exhibition

Children should be introduced to science in the primary school. Only then they would be able to understand and appreciate the beauty of science in higher classes. In the primary school, hardly any physics or chemistry is introduced to the students. Children are introduced to nature, hygiene, plant life and animal life. The exposure to science that children receive in primary school is confined to environmental science. Very few teachers make it interesting.

During a class visit to Standard I the students were questioned as to why the plants kept near the window inside the class room were growing outside the window. One of the students answered, "The plant is trying to go out because tomorrow is a holiday." Sweet as it may sound, it was a display of utter lack of scientific reasoning for which the teacher who introduced the project of "growing plants inside rooms" should be held responsible.

In our school we put up an excellent science exhibition by the primary school children. We called it "Alice in Science land". Nearly 120 students welcomed the chief guest with a dance. As soon as the chief guest cut the ribbon, two students dressed as Alice and Mr.Rabbit stopped her, enacting a scene from the book, *Alice in Wonderland*. Then, the guest came straight to Newton who was sitting under an apple tree explaining the law of gravity. We had selected a student who could not speak English well in order to give him a chance to discover himself. The boy was so overwhelmed by his role that he spoke his lines throughout the three hours non-stop without making any mistake about the law of gravity.

The wig and the dress suited him perfectly well. I do not know if the boy would ever remember how much faith the Principal had in his capabilities. His mother and I will always remember the fact that he was the main attraction of the science exhibition.

After encountering Newton the chief guest was directed to what was called as "unscientific corner" where tarot readers and witches sat with crystal balls. Then she faced a galaxy of scientists starting from early man inventing fire to Kalpana Chawla, the astronaut. Then the Chief Guest witnessed a mini rocket take off!

The students of Std I demonstrated the phenomenon of stimuli and effect. A student who dressed as Sun would glide across the hall slowly. Other students wearing masks of sunflowers turned their faces towards the moving student. The "sunflowers" drooped as the "Sun" set.

Some students put up a puppet show on Archimedes principle. Students themselves narrated the story of how Archimedes ran shouting "Eureka" and explained the principle.

Some others created a village scene where a farmer and his wife explained various types of "Land formations."

Some students converted their classroom into a beach. There were an aquarium, coconut trees and sand bed on which mermaids sleepily lazed about. A movie, "Finding Nemo "was shown on an LCD screen. Parents were given two tasks. One was a treasure hunt—to find a soft toy of Nemo which was hidden in the school premises. The other task was to answer science questions posed by a pirate at knife –point! The pirate would hand over a prize to those who answered questions correctly.

Some students put up a show called "Date with Mowgli". A jungle was created in the class room. Students appeared in costumes that represented the various stages of the metamorphosis of a caterpillar into a butterfly. A student dressed up as a caterpillar explained the metamorphosis. Mowgli would appear in the scene every now and then to entertain the guests.

Students had enacted a play wherein two street urchins kill a passerby and his skeleton returns to haunt them elaborating details about bones.

Some students spoke about volcanoes both dormant and active. They had made a model of a volcano which erupted (on adding turmeric and soda)! They called their project "Fire on the mountains".

There was also a show, Babbage & Babbage conducted by a parent-child team. The visitors to their stall answered a quiz on astronomy and witnessed working models of lungs. It is worth noting here that many teachers were educated by the students that day that it was Charles Babbage who invented computers and that his son, Henry Babbage, pursued the work of his father.

The science exhibition was a grand success. Students and teachers were simply thrilled with their own innovativeness. The parents were stunned and wanted a repeat show of the exhibition on the following day for the benefit of the general public. I was numbed by the exhilarating experience which was the best ever in my life. I was impressed with the teachers for having made the children take so much interest in science. LCD screens fixed in every classroom by the management showing the above scenes added a new dimension to the success of the science exhibition.

I am sure many schools organize similar and better science day celebrations.

Graffiti by students

The front wall of our school faced a busy road. It often invited posters and undesirable graffiti by the passers-by. Rather than confront the offenders, we thought it fit to engage the students in exhibiting their own artistic abilities to sketch graffiti on this wall. The children would dip their palms in colour and imprint them on the wall which resulted in attractive designs. The art and craft teacher patiently and enthusiastically guided them.

Dress code for the staff

I had introduced a dress code for teachers. Teachers would wear Indian and western outfits on alternate days. On Fridays they could wear dresses of their choice. The initial resistance on the part of the teachers was overcome after I explained the advantages of uniforms for teachers.

They were provided by the school.

They looked totally in command, serious and formal.

They stood out in a crowd as teachers of the school, distinct from visitors—easy to identify and could be approached by anyone who had any query about the school.

It saved them precious time in the mornings when generally they had confusion as to what to wear for the day!

Teachers and their better halves

A teachers' job is never taken seriously even by her family members. During festivals and functions at home, she would be expected to take a day off from school (however important her duty at the school be) and not the husband. After all a day's salary of the teacher at the school will be less than that of the husband at the office.

To make the husbands of the teachers of our school appreciate the importance that the school accorded to the teachers we invited them for a get-together. The credit entirely goes to one of the trustees who supported this idea and sponsored the programme. The teachers arrived at the venue beaming with their husbands. The husbands realized the importance of the work done by their wives at school and appreciated that the school valued the teachers enormously. Few would have any doubt as to who the better half was.

An experiment before summer vacation

Upon completing the annual examinations and announcing the results in March, many schools would conduct classes for a month before the summer vacation. In our school, the term began in April and extended till May. We decided to do things differently in our school as this one month stood in isolation for various reasons.

a) New entrants to school would be admitted in the summer breaks. So, starting with the syllabus would mean repetition for them once the school reopened in June.

b) Even if the actual teaching started, the students would forget everything when they came back from the summer vacation.

c) Mumbai experiences extreme sultry weather in summer. Epidemics and water borne diseases would be on the rise. Many students would miss school.

Keeping the interest of students in mind, we decided to

- keep the text books away for that month;
- teach only basic grammar and hold language enhancing classes like creative writing etc.
- provide intense training in improvement of basic mathematics skills and computations.

During the first three or four periods at the beginning of the day teachers engaged the students in the above mentioned areas with all seriousness. We divided the entire school, including the teachers, into five teams. Each team was assigned the responsibility to prepare for the celebration of important days such as Science Day, Mathematics Day, National Integration Day, International Day and Literary day. Usually in most schools, preparations for events are made during the academic term. That usually interferes with the school time-table.

The advantage of dividing the school into teams was that students of different age groups came to work together. Teachers got an opportunity to work with a vertical cross—section of students of the school. By the first break, all the teams would assemble in different venues and start preparing for the celebrations assigned to them. The teachers were made responsible for their respective teams. Enthusiasm spread to everyone. The time allotted was spent usefully and productively to put up a good show. By 12.30 PM the school wound up. This did not result in losing much on academics because even on regular school days, only activities such as Music, Art and Drama would take place after 12.30 PM.

For celebration of Science Day and Mathematics Day, students involved themselves in research, making models and preparing quizzes etc. For the National Integration Day student groups did research, practiced dances and made preparations for organizing a food festival of different states. The same was the case with International Day—students performed dances, served food of various countries, spoke about languages and culture, tourist attractions etc.

Literary Day was the culmination of celebratory events. It was held in the evening of the last day before the summer break. The DEAR (Drop Everything And Read) programme had had a significant effect on the students and the support staff by then. Students said they wanted to read their own poems rather than those of well-known poets!

Every day parents were invited to the school to participate and also witness the result of the month's work undertaken by their precious little ones. The parents were thrilled to see the amazing work done by the teachers and their children. The knowledge that the children gained in terms of academics was great. What was even greater was the improvement in their social skills, sense of belonging and sense of pride in being an important part of exciting projects like these.

The week began with a bang and ended on the last day with "poetry reading at Bon Fire". I started the programme reading my own poem about the school. The children had inspired me to write. This was followed by many enthusiastic young poets who recited their own poems in Hindi and English. The show was stolen by a couple of support staff. They came confidently on the stage to read poems. They faced the audience much better than most of the professional speakers would do. One of them even introduced herself to the audience in fluent English. The support staff had by then been trained into greeting appropriately and saying "Thank you". We felt that they should have a working knowledge of English as they were part of an international school.

When "Dreams" saw the light of day

It was always my dream to encourage the children to publish a school magazine. The editorial board comprised some students from Standards VI and VII and teachers of Hindi, French and English. We named the magazine "Dreams".

The children wanted to include in the magazine interviews of the neighbours. The children would visit the municipal garden in front of the school building as we did not have a play ground of our own. The teachers would briefly hold up the traffic on the busy road so that children could cross the road and reach the garden safely. The children used one such visit to the garden to interview some people there. The students of the editorial team asked a regular visitor to the garden if the school children disturbed them when they were relaxing at the garden. The gentleman replied," I did not even know that a school existed here. You are all so well behaved and disciplined and hardly create noise pollution in a residential place like this. Thanks for interviewing me. I feel honoured".

The Hindi teacher shifted the environment from the class room to the garden so that the children would be inspired to write poems which were later published in the magazine. The magazine provided an opportunity for the creativity of the students to blossom.

After considerable efforts put in by everyone in the school finally the first magazine of the school, "Dreams", was released on the annual day.

Peaking performance of students and staff

When school life is packed with exciting activities, every day children, teachers and the support staff would experience something new and interesting. Indiscipline would never raise its ugly head for the simple reason that the students and teachers would be engaged in academic pursuits. This would drive boredom away from learning or teaching.

A consultant was appointed for EIP (English Improvement programme) for teachers. Once she accompanied us for a school picnic.

She wrote in her article for Dreams:

> "—there was a spirit of camaraderie and a rare informality that crossed the Principal-staff gap. Silly jokes, riddles were traded and confidences exchanged— a tribute to the ease that Mrs. Nandakumar could establish, when needed, with her staff. This is important but rare; for often this relationship of staff with the Principal is one of formal distance or one of fawning attention."

When innovations are encouraged in schools teachers definitely contribute to the school's progress. They become more sincere and hard working. They display enthusiasm. They realize their self-worth by properly utilizing the freedom that is not curtailed by the Principal and the Management.

The introduction of excitement in education produced significant results. For the students, teachers and the support staff it was a pleasure coming to school. Parents were happy and contented with the progress their wards had made in the school.

Establishing a name for our school in a locality where there was competition from reputed schools posed many challenges. Our team of teachers contributed in seminars and workshops. Other schools noticed our teachers and me in seminars and workshops. Three or four articles appeared in the newspapers within a short period.

There are many schools that are engaged in similar creative activities.

In our school the entire team did dedicated work.

The management supported it.

The parents appreciated it.

The students deserved it.

CHAPTER 13
PUNCTUALITY IN SCHOOLS

Never too late

Punctuality signifies the respect one has for others' time and also one's own time. We teach punctuality to students but often teachers, Principals and the trustees fail on this front. A school functions within the structured framework of a time table. The class hours, tests and various school activities are determined after a lot of consideration and thought. For the smooth-running of a school punctuality is essential. Which place is better suited to inculcate the culture of punctuality in the young ones than the school? However, chaos reigns supreme in many schools due to lack of punctuality on the part of the management, the Principal, the teachers and the students. The students would be the first to correct themselves, if the issue is addressed properly.

Heads of Organizations and punctuality

I found lack of punctuality the biggest negative quality of our people. I am talking about adults: Teachers, Principals, Directors and Trustees of schools. I was called for an interview for the post of Principal at 3.30 pm. I reached 15 minutes before time but was not called in for nearly one hour. I reminded the clerk twice but the school authorities were simply chatting away. Finally after waiting patiently for a couple of hours I got an opportunity to interact with the school authorities. I was selected out of 250 candidates! This is how a prospective Principal of the school is treated by the school authorities.

Persons who are invited for the interview for the post of Principal have to go through a series of doors, enter their names in registers at the entrance, collect a visitor's card given to them and wait endlessly. This is a common practice observed in many places of work. People at the top of the hierarchy feel that they will be respected only if visitors are made to wait endlessly. I was faced with an instance where the Chairman of the Board of Trustees of an international school proudly announced that she would never be on time for any event and it was deliberate.

The Chairman of a reputed international school who had once invited me for an interview for the post of Principal, made me wait for four hours before calling me in. Another candidate who was also waiting along with me demanded that we both be served coffee during the long waiting period! I wonder what kind of treatment I would have got if I had become the Principal of such a school.

Only in one school the Principal called me in exactly at the time of appointment and without wasting any time asked me if I could join her school. This itself was indicative of the work culture of the school.

Teachers and Punctuality

The students would never like to be questioned about the reason for their late coming in front of their class mates. If

146

they were questioned, they would give some lame excuses like "Mom asked me to wait for the milkman", thereby indirectly revealing the contempt the parents had for punctuality! I decided to close the class room door after the second bell rang. Late comers were not allowed to enter the class room. In a few days the situation started improving. They realised that it was their turn to request their mothers to literally push them out of their beds so that they arrived on time for my class. *It is always easy to bring the students to conform to the rules.*

The students of a school where I worked would often say that they did not come on time because there was no teacher in the class room! I was given a class in the first period on **all** days. I did not mind it at all but the problem was that other teachers were not punctual.

My students and I were always on time but the other classes were noisy as their teachers arrived late. No teaching was possible because of the noise made by the students in the class where the teacher had not arrived on time. After tolerating this disturbance for a few months, one day I complained to the Principal about the rest of the classes disturbing me though we were on time. The Principal was furious and turned towards the entrance only to see half a dozen teachers sauntering in late. He demanded an explanation from them for being late. There was chaos in the staff room. Normally one has heard of "two wrongs do not make a right" but in this case there were many wrongs but only "one right". One teacher came in support of the late comers. She said teachers will come on time provided the Principal stopped conducting coaching classes. Mixing up issues with a dash of veiled accusation is a diversionary strategy. The defaulting teachers could effectively side-track the issue of punctuality.

My first step after I took over as the Principal of a new International School was to address the issue of late coming by students, teachers and support staff. Since the support staff would never arrive on time the school gates were never opened on time. I would arrive at the school on time and wait for the support staff who would report for work late to open the gate. I faced this problem on the first two days. On the third day as I saw no one in the premises in the morning, I got frustrated and disappointed and decided to return home. On the way back home I rang up the trustees and informed them that in spite of my best efforts to come to school on time, I was prevented from entering the premises. This must have prompted the trustees to act. The support staff from then on came on time. I would reach the school 30 minutes before time and welcome the students and teachers. Everyone started coming on time.

Even in schools where transport is organized by the management, students and teachers arrive late. In another school where I worked as Principal, the management had arranged for vehicle to ferry the teachers to the school from a defined rallying point. I exhorted the teachers to be punctual and stressed the importance of being thoroughly professional. Obviously, teachers did not take my advice seriously. I observed that despite the pick—up facility the teachers arrived late. They, however, blamed the driver for reporting late.

It turned out that the driver was not responsible for the delay. The late-coming teachers would telephone the teachers who had reached the rallying point on time, to wait until they arrived there. It is puzzling that teachers who reached the rallying point on time kept silent. Annoyingly in many places of work the wrong doers outnumber those who are right. The decent ones are small in number and afraid of confronting the defaulters. They are too decent to protest! When they outnumber the other group, things will start working better.

The driver was instructed to leave the rallying point at the assigned time and not to wait for the late-comers. The effect of these measures was observed immediately. Every person reported on time.

Students and punctuality

Punctuality should be ingrained in students by the school and by the parents. In the first few days after I joined as the Principal of a school I observed that the students seldom came to school on time. Initially, the students reported late because the buses would leave the school late in the morning to pick up the students. Bus loads of students would reach the school late. This was possibly the result of the trend set by the unpunctual teachers.

There was a need to put an end to this practice. The sports teachers were appointed at the entrances for checking the late-comers. Students' council members and traffic squads were constituted to check the late comers. Slowly everyone started coming on time. Students who came by private cars were allowed inside the school compound only if they came on time. Remarks were entered in the diaries when students arrived late. The results were noticeable! The students reported to school on time emulating their teachers who were now punctual!

CHAPTER 14
TEACHER ABSENTEEISM

Teacher, the mother

Teachers in many schools are all ladies. Few men opt to become teachers. Men prefer to teach higher classes. It is rare to find male teachers in primary schools.

An important, if not the most important reason for teacher absenteeism in schools is teachers going on maternity leave. After all a vast majority of school teachers are ladies. As far as the teacher is concerned it is not possible to balance one's time between school and a new born child. It is not fair on either. How would a teacher do an important assignment at school as the supervising examiner on a day when her child is running temperature at home? She would compromise on her motherhood, on her duties as a teacher and also her own well-being. This is a challenge faced by teachers today. Of late, there are schools which grant maternity leave for a year and promise to keep the teachers on their roll for the leave period so that they could take care of the children without worrying about their career.

The Government of India offers three years of paid leave for mother care which can be availed any time until the child becomes a major. Three cheers to the Government of India!

It is a matter of professional responsibility for a teacher to discharge her duties in the school without any hindrance. It is the emotional responsibility of the mother to stay at home and provide the much needed attention to the new born even if there is someone else at home. That someone else at home is not *the* one that matters most to the child. The child is the responsibility of only the women in India.

Many teachers are prepared to come back after three months of maternity leave. The students are left in the lurch as it is difficult to find a teacher for just three months. The quality of teaching suffers. While in any working environment, such absence by an employee would affect the overall performance, in a school, students would suffer acutely by such absence because of the time bound nature of the academic terms of the school. The solution may be that *the teacher should take a longer leave—minimum one year*.

Many senior women teachers or Principals are burdened with responsibilities towards post delivery care of their daughters or daughters-in-law. They have to absent themselves from school for long durations of time and if they are going overseas the duration could be 6-8 months.

House holding the teacher at home

Another reason for teacher absenteeism is that teachers want to go on long leave even foregoing the salary for the period, to join their husbands working abroad. Some teachers go on extended vacations. Undertaking pilgrimage is another reason. Festivals, weddings in the family and even certain domestic issues would prompt them to remain absent from work. The woman teacher gets no relief at home. Probably the other family members feel that she is after all a low paid teacher or a woman for whom home should come first.

Absenteeism of female workers may be common in other professions too impacting profit and loss but in the case of the teaching profession *the entire loss due to teachers' absenteeism is borne by the students!*

More men should take to teaching profession. With some schools offering the Sixth Pay Commission pay scales, including medical insurance, canteen facilities, transport facilities, etc. teaching profession is now slowly becoming attractive.

One cannot quantify the loss suffered or the set back experienced by the children when one teacher is substituted by another. Therefore the loss gets ignored!

Santosh Desai, a journalist, in his article in the Times of India, dated 3 March 2011, says that once a group of working women were asked whether their companies gave them extra support when they went on maternity leave. Only three or four hands (out of 300) went up. This was during a seminar that coincided with the International Woman's day.

More and more countries are including men in the ambit of childcare benefits to correct the skew that exists in many societies that makes childcare an exclusively female responsibility. An Indian husband would not hesitate to change nappies of his new born baby while living outside India but would stop the practice once he steps on the Indian soil. Cultural differences could be the reason. This mind set has to change. The idea of work needs to change as women are becoming an integral part of the world even outside the home.

With traditional family support disintegrating fast, the society needs to ensure that children, who are the citizens of the future, need to be groomed and looked after well. This is where the state needs to frame rules and policies for proper care of children.

The existing system needs to change radically.

CHAPTER 15
LACK OF CO-ORDINATION IN SCHOOLS

Good schools and great schools

Some good schools suffer due to lack of coordination among the constituent entities. One such school, accords due importance to academics, sports, co-curricular activities and most importantly culture. All the students and the staff of the school greet one another with a smile every morning. The school emphasises on grooming the students well. However, in their day-to-day activities there is no coordination among them and the result is a general chaos. The school, therefore, remains merely a *good* school. It would be a *great* school, if only the different components of the school worked in close coordination. This is true of many good schools.

These schools have earned a reputation because the school management takes enormous efforts towards

- induction of new teachers
- documentation of details of all school activities
- infrastructure to teachers and students and
- facilitating professional development courses for their teachers.

If the need for creating and sustaining a system that assures continuous coordination among the staff is not recognized, a school faces many problems.

Lack of co-ordination in transport service

The teachers *should* coordinate between the children and the transport operator to ensure that all the children safely board the bus and no one is left behind. In the above-mentioned good school the teachers would leave the school before the children did. On my first day as the Principal of the school, just as I was preparing to leave the school in the evening, I noticed two students huddled in a corner near the gate. They had missed the school bus. Everyone had left the school by then. I contacted their parents, stayed back with the students until the parents came and picked them up. After this incident, I always made sure that the child who missed the school bus sat just in front of me in my office till the parents came. Lack of supervision can pose a serious threat to the safety of students.

One day, a practice session for a school event was in progress. All students who did not participate in that event were asked to remain in the class. There was no proper supervision of these children. One of them, a little boy, boarded the wrong school bus in the evening.

The boy did not reach home at the usual time. The alarmed parents came rushing to the school and reported the matter to me. A search party was sent all over the school. The boy was not to be seen. The mother was terrified and was in tears. Though I assured her that we would find her child soon, I heard my heart beat faster than usual. I tried to remain cool while all the time I was worried about the disappearance of the boy.

After thirty traumatic minutes, the boy appeared in my office accompanied by a stranger, who turned out to be a new bus driver. It emerged that on that day the transport operator had sent an extra bus with a new driver. This boy was the lone occupant of this extra bus as the other students had boarded their respective buses and left. As no one else boarded the bus the driver waited outside the school for 30 minutes and brought the boy to my room. We all heaved a sigh of relief. No one can ever fathom the tension and anxiety that parents go through during these moments. Worse is the case with the Principal who not only needs to be calm under such stressful moments and also has to think of immediate steps to find the missing child. No time should be lost. One wrong move by the Principal could spell disaster to the child and also the school.

All this could have been avoided if the teacher, the students and the transport staff had functioned in a coordinated manner. Teachers should be in charge of students all the time while in school. The teacher who was supposed to supervise these students should have been alert in ensuring that all the students boarded the respective buses.

Ineffective delegation of work

In principle, a school can function well if work is delegated to competent persons. In a school, the senior teachers would meet the Principal every morning to discuss the events that were planned for the day. In theory, it would appear to work well. In practice, it did not bear fruits because these teachers went about their tasks in a disjoint manner without coordination.

In a school which had functioned without a Principal for some time, the coordinators conducted the school without much understanding among themselves. They constantly gave direct feedback to the members of the management. They all congratulated each other on how successfully the school was functioning. Though they were given credit there were problems about the school's style of functioning. Because of the absence of a systematic approach, students would leave the school as per their parents' wish. Parents would get special permission to take away their wards from the teachers with whom they had good rapport. Tests started at different times and ended at different times in class rooms depending on the arrival of the teachers who were to supervise the tests.

This was the result of delegation of work to ineffective persons.

Unfortunately students were subjected to the incoherent functioning of the school.

Noise pollution in schools

In the schools in our country, it is a given that there would be noise. "Children *would* make noise" is how some of us see it. There are those who maintain "Children *should* make noise". The noise level inside the campus of our school was between 100 and 110 decibels as measured using a decibel meter. Even in industrial and commercial environment the limits on noise level are 75 dB and 65 dB respectively.

The health hazard due to increased levels of noise pollution includes impaired hearing, annoyance and deterioration of speech communication. Researchers in Cornell University in New York have suggested that children from noisy environs have poorer reading skills than those who come from quieter areas. (Source: http://old.cseindia.org/programme/health).

I spoke to the students about the harmful effects of noise pollution. I have, over the years, read that bus accidents happen frequently due to the noise made by passengers, marriage parties or picnic parties travelling in the bus. The noise level caused by them makes the driver lose his concentration and, therefore, control over the bus. It is a well known fact that constant exposure to excessive noise can cause severe injury.

A campaign against noise pollution was started by me and the students. The campaign fell on deaf ears. A good move to reduce noise pollution fell through because of lack of concerted effort by all concerned.

Management's interactions

Establishing schools is a noble deed. Many have ventured into providing education to children but very few have succeeded in keeping the focus on the children. Some look at it as a business venture, some as power wielding tools and some genuinely with the thought of making a contribution to the society. Even those who start schools with noble intentions often get derailed completely within a short period of time. This often affects the school's reputation. New schools are beset with teething troubles. The management sometimes directly gets involved in the day-to-day functioning of the school issuing instructions randomly to individuals. This leads to breakdown of coordination among the school staff and the Principal. When this happens there are no options left to the Principal or teachers except to leave the organisation. Some stick around as they have limited options and are forced to put up with the autocratic ways of functioning of the management.

It is necessary and even good that the management gets involved in the running of the school. Sometimes the management goes overboard and starts breathing down the neck of the Principal. Lack of coordination among the members of the management, comes in the way of the effective functioning of the school. Unnecessary delays, lack of focus and politics lead to incoherent actions and ruin the school's progress.

Parents are our stakeholders and their satisfaction should be our main agenda. This does not mean that you pamper parents and let them run the school entirely. The best way for the management to function is to get the teachers and the Principal to commit themselves to delivering quality education aligned with the philosophy of the management. The management should give them the necessary support and provide a favourable unfettered working environment conducive to effective functioning. This will eventually help the management see students progress, earn the goodwill of the parents and retain talented staff with the school.

It is not the pay packet alone that helps an organisation to retain its staff members. The work culture and the care and respect the management gives its staff contribute significantly. This along with a decent package will ensure that the school is run efficiently without attrition.

In some schools facilities such as a decent pay packet, accommodation and medical assistance are extended to the teachers. While all this is necessary for teachers it is not sufficient to ensure commitment and accountability on the part of the teachers.

Sometimes the management interferes so heavily with the school that the focus of the Principal and staff is shifted away from the children.

The managing trustees of our school appointed a consultant from abroad to advise them on school matters. He started interfering with the smooth functioning of the school introducing incoherency in the teachers' actions. We did not realize at first that the consultant had his personal agenda in bagging the assignment with the school. After interacting with the consultant, I submitted a report to the trustees on his unprofessional way of handling the school affairs. The studied inaction on the part of the trustees was intriguing.

Generally, the Principal would participate in the periodic meetings organized by trustees. With the arrival of the consultant my participation in the meetings got curtailed. The Principal should not be called in to participate in meetings midway and asked to leave before the meeting ended, except when her presence was not required for the meeting.

The consultant was not based in India. He hardly knew the ground realities of running schools in India. In addition, he had no experience in heading schools in India or abroad. He had no teaching experience. In spite of all these drawbacks, the management suddenly decided that the consultant would supervise the Principal.

My teaching staff and I strongly felt that all of us were working to cross purposes. I decided to resign citing personal reasons for quitting. If the management which runs the school stands firmly by its faltering steps, it can be very de-motivating for the teachers and particularly for the Principal. One fails to understand what exactly they expect from their own employees. If they are not clear as to what their goal is, they will interfere with their staff destructively rather than interact constructively. Can the staff ever give of their best to the organisation under such interference?

When the staff members are able to see things falling apart because of the faulty policies and decisions taken by the management that disrupted the coordinated efforts of the team, one wonders why the management is unable to see clearly the downfall of their school.

CHAPTER 16
THE MANAGEMENT

Management of reputed schools

As a rule reputed schools retain their Principals for a long period of time and this helps enhancing the school's image and passing on the culture to new entrants into the school—be it a new teacher or a student or a support staff. They are proud to declare that they are part of an organisation of repute. Such a school is like a branded commodity and its employees brand ambassadors. Here the Principals are accorded the due freedom and treated with dignity. The management relies more on the judgement of the Principal as the latter knows the pulse of the people involved in the school better than anyone else. At no point the Principal's authority gets undermined. Just as a Principal cannot undermine the teachers' authority in the class room, the Principal's authority should not be undermined by the management in public view.

Management and the school system

A school management should ideally appoint a well qualified and experienced person to head the organisation designated as Head / Director / CEO. The appointment of the Principal should be the next step. With the help of the Principal the CEO should carefully select competent teachers as coordinators for different sections of the school. It is important that the members of this team—the CEO of the organisation, the Principal and the coordinators understand the philosophy and culture of the organization. They form the core team and there should be transparency in the way they function. Every one's role should be defined and responsibilities allotted. This way they will not stray into each other's domain. In case they have some issues among themselves it would be advisable that they discuss and settle amicably so that the school does not get affected.

The CEO who decides to remain in the campus all the while will directly get involved in all matters concerning the school—preparation of the time table, staff meetings, appointment of teachers, etc. The CEO should have overall say in all these matters no doubt but day-to-day dabbling in individual matters would be inefficient. Handling of day-to-day matters should be the responsibility of the Principal. Details as to individual sections should be sorted out between the Principal and the coordinators.

If the CEO directly interacts with the coordinators and teachers, the consequences can be harmful. For example, the coordinators and the teachers will directly take permissions and sanctions from the CEO.

Teachers will be hired and fired at will by the CEO or the coordinators thereby sidelining the Principal.

Part time teachers will walk in and out of the school.

The Principal will be left to complete tasks that neither the CEO nor the coordinators are willing to do.

Frequent change of the Principal would become the norm. Such changes would introduce instability to the school. This is evidenced by the fact that in reputed schools the Principal is not changed frequently, as noted elsewhere.

In such a set up the Principal would be the weakest link. The net result would be utter chaos. The school's reputation would get affected in the long run.

If such chaos has to be avoided, it is essential that clarity is established in the responsibilities of the CEO, Principal and coordinators and duly implemented.

Management and Principal

In the earlier days the Principal was all in all—a single point of contact between the school and the management. Her authority was never questioned in front of her staff. Decisions on day-to-day matters were made by the Principal and they were accepted as such. The trustees remained in the background though they effectively controlled the running of the school in consultation with the Principal.

Nowadays in some schools the Principals are pre-occupied with only their own performance. They function completely oblivious of other schools in the region. They do not interact with other schools. They even encourage inner and outer circles to develop among the staff members of their schools thereby losing touch with their own staff and students.

A change has come over the Principal's role in schools.

During the interview for a Principal's post, the members of the management tell the candidate that she, as Principal, represents the management and that they will honour her decisions. In practice, they would exclude the Principal from decision making. On the one hand, they would tell the Principal to be nice to the parents and on the other, worry that the Principal might be gaining popularity among the parents. They would encourage parent's complaints against the Principal and teachers and demand explanations from the Principal.

The Principal would be left wondering if she was in-charge of the school at all. Instead of sitting with the Principal and briefing her about the policies and strategies of the school they would let her handle situations and get information from other quarters. This would leave many Principals wondering whether their efforts were being recognised at all by anyone. Many of the Principal's serious and sincere suggestions would go unnoticed. The Principal is reduced to being just a mediator between the parents and the management on the one hand and the teachers and the management on the other, *with the students getting pushed into a blur*!

If the leader is constantly scrutinised, supervised and admonished for things that, as perceived by the management, go wrong, how will the leader be able to motivate the team members? In situations requiring immediate action, the Principal is left in a dilemma as to whether to act quickly relying on her experience and inform the management later or to wait and seek the management's permission before acting. If the Principals act independently, the management's ego would be hurt. If the Principals seek advice from the management they would be criticised for not acting promptly. It is like asking a fellow to participate in a race after tying up both feet.

It is not even remotely suggested that Principals should have total free hand in the matters relating to the running of the school. What is recommended here is that the zone of operation of the Principal should be defined and that the Principal should be allowed to operate unfettered within the defined space with responsibility and accountability so that she is not blamed for consulting or not consulting the management before making any decision. The Principal has to implement the policies of the trust and should be enabled to do so with dignity.

CHAPTER 17

THE PARENTS

Parents are an integral part of the school. When they admit their ward to the school they indirectly sign a contract with the school authorities that at the end of schooling their ward would have achieved all round development. They support the school by way of fees and direct participation in the school events. *Most parents* fulfil their role as brand ambassadors of the school. A few parents cause disturbance to the tranquillity of the school. The school, on its part, should honour and address genuine complaints made by the parents.

Discipline comes from home. Some parents feel that rules can be bent in favour of their wards. The child gets a signal that the parents will come to their rescue and bail them out of trouble, whenever needed. If the undisciplined go scot free, then the other students get a clear message that they can do anything and get away with it. Such incidents should be handled with sensitivity. Parents have a huge responsibility in this context.

Parents-ambassdors of the school

Parents are important for any school. Their voices should be heard at all times. In our school we made sure that parents felt that our school was the right one for their wards. Some steps taken by the school were—

A page was dedicated on the website of the school for the parents. Their feedback in their own hand writing was scanned and uploaded on their page every week.

We made them part of the school celebrations.

On the sport's day the teachers' teams had organised tug-of-war with the parent's team. It is pointless to recall who won. After all don't they both together form a winning team for the school?

When we changed the uniform of the children the choice was made by the parents through a process of voting.

All these measures which were introduced to take the parents on board helped in the smooth functioning of the school.

Bringing up the parents.

In a school, a conscientious teacher, pulled up her students for unsatisfactory performance in the class tests. The girls of a junior class had to face the wrath of the teacher for faring poorly in the tests. The teacher might have used some harsh words for which the students thought of *teaching the teacher a lesson*. They wrote a hate-letter using abusive words on a social net working site. The teacher was shocked at this incident. The girls were summoned to my office.

I asked them "How could you do this? You used those words in spite of knowing the meaning? What would your mother think of you if she got to know about what you did? Will you confess to your mother?"

One girl said yes and the other said no. The girl who said yes said "My mother will scold me but that does not bother me because she has every right to scold me." The girl, who said no, muttered "There is no point in telling her because she will not be able to believe that *I* did this. I don't want to let her down by confessing this incident to her". They spoke the plain truth.

Parents have to do a lot towards building the character of their children. The students were made to understand that the teacher did not deserve this from her students. After all she had high expectations from her students, which was good. If they had objections to her methods they could have spoken to the teacher directly instead of resorting to these undesirable ways. I asked "If these same words were used by any of the teachers on you how would you feel?" They agreed that they would have taken offence if anyone had used such words about them.

The girls seemed to be relieved that they were given a patient hearing. They were not shouted at or the Principal did not get angry with them. They felt ashamed of their behaviour. They realized that the teacher was treated badly by them.

Later the teacher confirmed that they apologized. I knew they genuinely regretted their action. This incident only tells us how difficult it must be for the parents to bring up children. The students of this generation are prone to getting misguided. Schools need to correct the errant children with great sensitivity.It is the parents' responsibility to correct the children. The school has to support the parents.

Instances of students physically attacking Principals and teachers have been reported. Students misuse social networking sites and MMS to spread negative messages about the school, other students, teachers and the Principal. It may not take long before such incidents become more frequent. Lack of parental care is cited as a major reason for such abnormal incidents.

Parents' attitude towards schools

Students make their journey to school in the morning hours peacefully. Some are sleepy and the rest probably look forward to excitement in school. Their return journeys are not as peaceful as the onward trip.

Once, while going home in the evening in the school bus a boy from a junior class was beaten up by two senior boys. Even if the younger boy had misbehaved with the older ones (which is very unlikely), the seniors were not right in harming him.

The parents of both students were informed about this incident. One set of parents verified the facts and expressed regret over their son's actions. The parents of the other senior boy came to school with a letter stating that their son was innocent and ought not to have been blamed. They claimed that he never touched the child and was being blamed by the school baselessly. They added that he was in a senior class and was stressed because of the accusation.

The fact that one set of parents verified the facts and regretted the incident, called the bluff of the other parents. To blatantly lie was bad. To blame the school for causing stress to the child was worse and unfair on the school—even more so on the bruised junior. These parents diverted our attention from the incident by blaming the school for creating stress to their ward. *They missed an opportunity to correct their son.* After all the boys are young and we need to put right things into their heads. I appreciate the parents of the other errant student who acted in the interest of their son. Hats off to such parents! It is better to admit one's mistakes, rather than deny and offer counter arguments to justify wrong actions. What an example to set for the child to follow! It would certainly backfire on such parents and it would be too late to undo the harm they had done.

The first parent had trust in the school and therefore readily agreed to cooperate with the school. On the other hand the second parent denied the charge because of fear of the son being victimised by the school. This *trust deficit* between parents and school should be overcome.

The school has an important duty in assuring the parents that under no circumstances the child would be victimised and that only the child's behaviour would be corrected.

Responsible and irresponsible parents

In many schools, the parents are very supportive of the school. The way they volunteer during the sports day or any other function is praiseworthy. Many parents volunteer to help the school during functions. The Parent Teacher Association (PTA) of each school should be responsible and proactive.

In an incident, during the prelims of the Standard X, a student was absent. The office rang up his home only to find that the child was unwell. We requested for a medical certificate. The certificate was sent through the neighbour. We suspected that the parents were hiding something from us. We sent a letter to the child's home asking for further clarifications about his illness. The letter came back to us. The next day when we called the father, the student answered followed by the father himself. Some excuses were offered by both but what they did not realize was that even as our conversation with them was in progress, the announcements made in the railway station were clearly heard by us. Obviously the student was being taken by the parents out of station. Should the parents not be responsible towards the school that they patronise? What message are they sending to their own child?

Pushy parents and the adverse effects

In schools which are intended for and managed by a close community certain aberrations are witnessed. Since the children of all the employees of the organization go to the same school constant comparisons about the performance of the children woud be a topic of conversation among the parents. The boss may not like his subordinate's children doing better in academics than his own. The scene would get so vicious that students would not get out of their homes until the fever caused by board results subsided. The neighbours would express shock if any student scored less than 90% aggregate saying "Why did your son do so badly?" Worse still, they would openly tell the child about their shock. The child would then withdraw into a shell –refusing to show his/her face to anyone.

In one such school because parents gave undue importance to a career in engineering and medicine for their wards, they pushed their children to take up science stream. Any student opting for commerce or arts, was branded as no good. Some students did badly in their higher studies just because their parents would not accept anything less than an engineering degree or MBBS from their wards. They were simply not suited for these courses. They took more years than the minimum stipulated to pass the exams. Some students would go into depression because they got low marks in crucial Board Exams.

It is often the pushy parents and the nosy neighbours who put unhealthy ideas in the minds of children. These adults are a menace to the society.

Many students who were discarded by such parents and neighbours as "no good" do well in their career. The parents and teachers should see their talent and potential rather than their marks! People should be sensitive to their neighbours' children and not make remarks that hurt them!

Parents' and school teachers

Some parents talk poorly of teachers in front of their children. This would undermine the respect that the teacher commands over her students. The parents may, however, express their opinion about teachers to the school authorities privately.

In an incident a student was wrongly admonished by the teacher. The father after hearing of this incident told the son who was in Standard VII to boycot the teacher's classes if he is admonsihed wrongly in the class again. He said that he would deal with the consequences himself and that the son need not worry. Does this advice help the child, the teacher or the parent?

In another incident a parent, after attending a school function, refused to stand up for the national anthem and started walking even though it was announced that everyone must stand up for the national anthem. He obviously wanted to show that he was not bound by the announcements made by the school teachers. What he did not realize was that he was insulting our national anthem and *setting a bad example to the children including his own.* We could not stop him and by the time the national anthem got over he had left the school campus.

A parent was on excellent terms with some members of the school management. He wanted to observe the lessons of teachers. He would always find teachers below par as he thought that his children deserved better teachers. Teachers would resent being monitored all the time by parents.

Another parent never respected the school rule that the lift was not to be used by senior students. She would bring her daughter early just to make sure that she used the lift though the daughter was in a higher class. She thought her daughter was far above the average students. The daughter was a real gem but my concern was that constant wrong advice from her mother would encourage her into rebelling against the school rules, as she grew older.

Parents and the school diary

School rules remain in the diary and very few parents read or follow them. Some schools wake up suddenly to check the uniform, long hair, shoes, etc., on the last day of school. This laxity drives students and parents not to take school seriously! In our school we checked these things regularly. The students and parents would behave as though we were springing surprises at them, be it a ban on having long hair or improper shoes or uniform.

Much precious time was wasted in checking these things and listening to the excuses the students, or more often their parents offerred. We decided to have a quiz on the diary for the students of the primary school. It turned out be a big hit. It was great to see the enthusiastic students answer all the questions correctly. Sometimes they made up their own answers to every one's delight. As the students now knew what was said in the diary they had no difficulty in abiding by the rules.

Parents and the school menu

In many schools children are served heavy snacks at the first break. They have light lunch during the second break. In one school, parents would prepare snacks and send them at odd hours. This practice interfered with the classes. The support staff was forever passing the snack boxes to the students. The parents would be rude to them if they did not oblige. This interfered with the work assigned to the support staff, who in turn became inefficient. The parents did not realise this.

The funniest part was that parents would crowd up in front of the gate to see the "menu of the day" (with details of nutrition in the food to be served) put up on the board by the nutritionists of the school. They would even pass comments about the "menu". Did they think we were running a restaurant?

To make parents aware of the nutrition aspect of the food, we at the school, started putting up the same details as "The nutrition value of the food your child had *yesterday*". The crowd soon disappeared. They would come up with complaints on the quality, quantity or lack of taste of the food. The management was providing subsidy for the meal. The caterer genuinely cared for the children. Anyone would have expected the parents to be happy that they were spared the agony of preparing lunch for their wards who got fresh nutritious food in the school.

This one takes the cake!

Parents would bring expensive gifts for their ward's birthday. One parent spent Rs 1500-2000 on a huge cake. A circular had earlier been sent to all the parents to stop this kind of practice. Instead we suggested that they donate an amount to an NGO that worked for the welfare of underprivileged children.

In another incident, a parent landed in my office on his son's birthday with 50 odd ceramic mugs and cakes to be given to the classmates of his son. I prevented him from distributing gifts reminding him of the school circular. The parent got enraged and accused me of spoiling his son's birthday.

An excited mother wanted the school to give her the address list of students in her son's class so that she could invite the entire class for her son's birthday celebrations. We had to convince her that it was against the rule of the school and that we would not be able to share even the phone numbers of the son's classmates.

Forceful parents

Parents sometimes force the children to perform.– For example a first grader was brought straight from the hospital bed to attend an interview. Such was the anxiety of the parents to secure admission for their ward. It was horrifying to see the intravenous tube in his wrist when he came accompanied by his father. He was given admission as he deserved a seat in the school.

In another case the mother would force her son to learn every lesson by heart. The parents would demand to be informed about the portions/syllabus so that the tuition teacher could prepare the child beforehand. They would drag the poor sick child (running high temperature) for writing the unit tests and ask for permission to take the child away after the test. As the Principal, I advised them that the child should be resting at home in bed and that he would be allowed to write only if he was fit to remain the whole day in school. How anxiety over the child's education overtakes common sense these days!

Communication with parents

Many of the problems can be prevented if the parents are kept informed periodically about the school activities. The Principal should keep communicating with the parents through circulars. Frequent circulars from schools may irritate some parents but generally it helps to keep parents in the picture. Given below is one such circular letter that I sent to all the parents of the students in our school.

Dear parents,

A warm welcome to all of you for the second term of the academic year I have been wanting to share a few of my views with all of you. Hence this open letter.

The other day a parent walked out of the school with the child's report card. The child, oblivious of his performance, asked his mother 'What does A* mean, Mama?' I was overwhelmed with a strange feeling of joy. After all wasn't this I expected of every student? I was happy to note that the child had no clue about his excellent performance in all subjects and was doing his bit in school which came naturally to him. Well, upon hearing this I congratulated the mother for not 'pushing' the child. The mother appeared contented and the son was very happy and confident, both satisfied with the happenings in our school.

Well, not all the students get A*s. The question is: Does it matter? What difference would it make for the six year olds or the seven year olds when they were just learning a whole lot of things for the first time in school? Then one may ask, 'Why are grades given at all?' Only to indicate the area in which the child needs to improve on her/his previous performance but definitely not meant as a comparison between peers.

Important note to parents:

- There are individual differences between children.
- Parental pressure on children to 'perform' will only harm and not help children in the long run.
- Some parents are either worried about too much home work (that they end up completing the HW for their kids) or not enough of home work.
- Parents want international educational standards for their children but are not willing to accept the fact that the process of attaining such standards will take time.

- Some parents compare their child's performance with that of their friends' children. This creates unhealthy environment in school.
- Some parents seem only to be stressed about grades of their child whereas we are concerned about the social habits of all our children.
- Some parents are worried about the academic growth of their child but we are concerned about the 'overall growth' of each and every child.

Our academic programme is **not about**:

- cramming
- rote learning and reproducing in exams
- facing easy question papers with no thinking or less thinking
- depending on parents or tuition teacher
- being asked the same questions again and again in the exams
- learning English and maths merely as *subjects*, which will lead to a situation where a child is totally lost if an unseen passage appears in the English paper or a multiplication problem is given as completion of a grocery store bill.

Our academic programme is **all about**

- understanding lessons
- thinking logically
- expressing views and thoughts in their own words
- activity centred classes
- field trip oriented learning
- computer literacy

- emphasis on core subjects; English, Mathematics and Science
- setting question papers in different patterns each year
- teaching English, maths as skills rather than as subjects
- relating subjects to day-to-day life
- exposure to information about the world.

Five months ago the job of the Principal of our school seemed a daunting task but not so today—thanks to nearly 90% of the parents who are being supportive, helpful and happy with what is offered by the school. I have been getting positive feedback from these parents from time to time. I have been getting unconditional support from the trustees and the staff. The staff recently attended workshops on subjects like Environmental Management, Art and Design and Hindi. This has given them opportunities to interact with teachers of international schools. They show tremendous inclination to develop as professionals and need to be encouraged by all of us. Children are my greatest asset and I draw strength from them.

The Trustees offer international education at **affordable cost** and the Principal of the school has more than two decades of teaching experience in CBSE, ICSE Boards and in an International school. Hence the parents should leave the academics to the school to handle. It is our endeavour to better ourselves each year. Do expect further improvements next year.

(Vimala Nandakumar)
Principal

It is needless to say that the rapport between the school and the parents improved because of such letters. The willing support offered by the parents was the USP of that school.

Parents and sports

Two days for sports are looked forward to with great eagerness by the sport enthusiasts among students and parents. Keeping in view of the humid weather of Mumbai, Sports Days are organised in the last week of December before the Christmas holidays. While most of the parents look forward to the sports week, some secretly plan to take off on holidays during the sports days together with the Christmas vacation. Some parents who are tempted to do so find it fit to inform the Principal about the secret plans of other parents.

Normally schools do not take any action against students (actually parents) for absenting themselves from school either without informing or on false pretexts. Parents seem to feel that missing the Sports Day is of no consequence. It is these very parents who would lecture to us about the importance of sports and playgrounds in schools at the time of securing admission for their wards in the school.

In order to discourage absenteeism on Sports Days we sent a circular to all the parents informing them that attendance was compulsory and that there would be some kind of consequences for those who miss the same.

We faced two different sets of reactions to the circular. Majority of those who planned holidays amended their plans. One couple landed at my office to request me to reconsider the proposal and allow them to take their daughter (of Standard I) to a pilgrimage as a group of relatives had booked their tickets. I told them that they should have checked the school diary before booking and that it was not right to inform me *post facto*. I firmly said that I would not give permission for the child to miss the Sport's Day and that they were free to do what suited them best. The parents were very decent and agreed that they would not undertake the journey. All the tickets were cancelled without any ill feeling or protest. We remembered to mention the names of the parents and spoke very highly about them on the annual day of the school.

In another incident, a grandparent quietly took away the grandson on a grand holiday to Bangkok. On his return he met me to explain the reason for the absence of the child on the Sports Day. He said that I should appreciate his honesty in admitting the fact that they had gone for a holiday to Bangkok instead of producing a false medical certificate. I asked him why he did not do so. He feared that since children were very honest his grandson might let the cat out of the bag thereby exposing the grandfather! Such contrast in the behaviour of parents make me wonder as to what kind of message they were sending to the young ones? Can we blame children for their misbehaviour? After all won't the children reflect the upbringing given by their parents in the school?

Thanks to the support of the trustees we asked parents who were defaulters to pay a fine not to the school but to an NGO working for the welfare of underpriveleged children. We justified this act by telling them that these children did not have the benefit of even basic education. They paid up because they knew that the school was right.

Parents' interest in their wards' achievements

It is natural that parents display interest in the achievements of their wards. They may force their eagerness on their children who would enjoy schooling without the excessive enthusiasm of the parents. Taking an active interest in the child's education often explodes into overenthusiasm on the part of the parents. This is infectious among parents. The overall impact on children is negative. In our school, we had made a promise to all the parents that we would invite their children to come up on stage for special reasons. We declared the day of results as "Special day". That was the last open day of the year and was held in a private auditorium. We placed the report cards in envelopes and sealed them. We attached certificates of good traits shown by children such as being punctual, registering improvement in academics, being well turned out and leadership qualities to the sealed envelopes. This was kept a secret from parents.

That day the auditorium wore a festive look. Parents, eager to know the grades of their wards attended in large numbers. In my speech I dwelt upon the importance of holistic development of the child. Academic excellence was only a part of a child's development. Social skills and exposure to sports played equally important parts in a child's life in school.

Generally parents read the report cards of their wards and compare them with those of the other children. This is not a healthy practice. We requested the parents to open the envelopes at home to see the grades and appreciate their children for their special qualities. The parents did exactly that. They were very happy because each child came up on the stage and was recognized for his/her special quality. The parents had trusted us and we justified their trust. It is then that we realized that we had won over the parents and had earned their unconditional support and respect.

Parents and school fees

School fees are generally determined by the Managing Trustees. The fees should be commensurate with the quality of schooling offered by the institution. It should be affordable for the parents whose children study in the school. When the fee is hiked, often parents resist the move. Even if the fee is reasonable as compared with that of a school of a similar profile, some parents resist.

The parents sometimes express their dissent by delaying the payment of the fees till the last date. After all, one can pay the fees "on or before" the specified date. The fees charged by our school were reasonable, probably the lowest among the 150 international schools in India at that time.

A reporter of a news magazine interviewed us and she was amazed at the low fees charged by us.

The trustees knew the financial impact of such low fees. Yet parents wanted some more concession. They all waited till the last date and crowded in front of the office, almost driving the administrative staff crazy. No one listened to the staff's pleas to stick to a queue. One of the Trustees rang me up and requested me to handle the chaos!

Still there were parents who sent students to the higher class without paying fees for the next academic year! This resulted in some embarrassment to the students. Why should the students be penalized for the fault of their parents? Why should they not pay the fees on time?

Once a parent of the school asked if some concession could be shown in the school fees as she was running short of money. When I prodded further to elaborate on the subject she said that she and her family were going to Australia for a holiday and therefore she was short of funds!

There are instances where parents are justified in protesting a fee hike. They only demand that the school offers all the promised facilities. In that case, they agree to the fee hike. Fee hike is another sensitive issue where parents should be taken into confidence *apriori*.

An angry parent vs Principal

Towards the end of the academic year when students were required to pay examination fees, the accounts department of our school repeatedly telephoned defaulters reminding them about the last date. They often told me that parents would speak rudely when they rang up to remind them. I had to intervene and personally call many parents. With a lot of delay and excuses the entire group of students paid up fees with fine except one. The student was probably terrified of the father and did not know how to get the fees paid. I rang up to remind the father.

The father screamed into my ears " Who are you to remind me about the fees? I will complain about you to the management. Just go to hell".

That was the first time I have ever heard such harsh words and was taken aback. I suppose good sense prevailed over me and I replied very calmly " If reminding you about fees will send me to hell, I don't mind going there. Please see that your son does not suffer because of your delaying the payment".

I realised later that the accountant came to me as the last resort to get her things done without getting yelled at by the parent. Within five minutes I faxed a letter to the administrator reporting the incident and copied it to the members of the management. I neither regretted complaining about him nor felt embarrassed that I was shouted at.

The payment of fees was done the next day, the accounts department could complete all formalities with the Board of Examination and the student could appear for the examination. The management did not interfere. I achieved my goal but swallowed the harsh words.

Now it hardly hurts.

Parent Teacher Meetings

The Principal, teachers, students and parents have their independent paths which meet, per force, on occasions. In some schools the Parent Teachers Meetings (PTM) are held rarely. In one of the schools, the science students were academically brilliant in contrast with students of the commerce stream who had no sympathy from school nor support from parents. The students of science stream thought it was below the dignity of their parents to visit the school during these days of PTM whereas the parents of the commerce stream visited teachers to find out if the children at least had a chance of improvement in studies and their behaviour in school.

Here are some tips for the parents to avoid a push that may become a shove.

How to be positive, not pushy

- Be positive and not excessively pushy
- Tust the school and support the school.
- Don't undermine the teachers.
- Never compare your children with other children including his/her siblings
- Do not try to realize your dreams through your child
- Be patient with the child

Parents and the school alike must appreciate the relevance and importance of assessing each other at regular intervals and interact positively so that the cause of education and the welfare of the students are duly addressed.

The responsibility that parents have in the running of the school where their wards study is monumental and should be discharged as a solemn social responsibility.

CHAPTER 18

FOREIGN ENTICEMENTS!

One sees advertisements in the newspapers and gets emails from head hunters about job opportunities for teachers and Principals overseas. Some of them are genuine but some have a tendency to entice the applicant by promising the Mars and at the last moment landing them on a marsh. The applicant gets so much "committed" to the position overseas that she/he accepts the final offer as it is too late to step back.

Once I was looking for a suitable opening in international schools. I was called for an interview by an educational institution. This institution was running international schools in many countries. They were looking for Principals and Vice Principals for their schools. According to the advertisement I could choose the country of my preference.

I chose Mauritius as my first preference and Thailand as the second. During my interview, one of the interviewers asked me if I would accept the Vice-Principal's post in another country. I declined the offer as I had already served as a Principal in schools. They said that my chances of getting a job could improve if I agreed to their suggestion. They said that they had a local candidate for their school in Thailand. Nothing was said about Mauritius. They told me that they would get back to me within a week. I could see that they lacked professionalism.

To my surprise, the very next day I got a call from them. I rushed thinking that I was selected as Principal of a school in the country of my choice. The administrator of the school in a country which was never mentioned by them before was waiting to tell me the terms and conditions they had to offer if I were to say "Yes" to the Principal's post in their school. I was hurried into going through the details of the pay and perks they offered. I was not sure whether their offer was good, considering the fact that living in that country would be an expensive proposition. In any case that country did not figure in their advertisement. I suspected that the people involved were totally disorganised because of the fact that they kept changing their stance every now and then. The advertisement said something and they offered something else. I rejected the offer as my gut feeling told me that I may not be able to function effectively in the hands of disorganised and unprofessional people.

In another instance, a highly qualified and experienced teacher was asked by an Indian institution to establish a new school in a country in South East Asia. As a thorough professional she asked the potential employers for clarifications on her role and responsibilities, the job profile and the package including medical facilities, accommodation and leave entitlement. They got offended (!) and withdrew the offer. The point is that even without her asking for these details, they should have mentioned all these details in their offer! It is not easy for a person to take up a big responsibility in a foreign land without any assurance or support from the employer. Such people continue to enrol children in their schools. This is an unprofessional approach. The trusting teachers are vulnerable to such enticements and apt to fall prey to such unethical practices. One wonders if these institutions are capable of focusing on children if selection of Principal was conducted in such an unprofessional manner.

By such enticements some good teachers leave the shores of our country and end up in difficult places. This way schools and students lose some good teachers.

The reasons for teachers to seek foreign assignments are:

1. Emoluments and higher potential to save
2. Working conditions
3. Educational opportunities for their children
4. Caring management
5. Transparency in dealings

These are the *expectations*. If all the above expectations are fulfilled, there is no case for a teacher to reject a foreign assignment. It would be value addition to her/his CV.

The teachers' emoluments in other countries may be better than in India. However, teachers are among the lowest paid employees in any country!

In reality some of the expectations come true and some do not. In a foreign land with the cultural gap to be bridged, many teachers, if not all, may find themselves like fish out of water. They realize that the overseas misadventure has interfered with their career. Often they end up being neither here nor there.

All this can be averted if only the educational institutions in India make it attractive enough for the teachers to work in India and not be enticed by foreign assignments.

CHAPTER 19
A DREAM SCHOOL

The chapters that the reader has come past constitute a description of the positives and the negatives of our schools to which the reader is no stranger. One is left wondering whether at all a school exists where the child is the focus –a dream school where true education comprising not only academics but also character building and personality development is imparted. It is indeed heart warming to observe that one such school does exist not far from the metropolis of Mumbai. Not long ago I had an occasion to visit the school.

The school was conducted by the wives of naval officers. There was a catering institute meant for the cadets of merchant navy in a sprawling beautiful campus. The officers' wives had the goodness not only to adopt the nearby villages where the inhabitants were almost entirely fisher folk but also to provide quality education to their children. Their initiative is indeed praiseworthy.

The ladies were keen that the children of the school got educated up to Standard X. Keen as they were to impart education to the village children, they held themselves from providing higher education in this school as the career ambitions of most of the students of the villages did not go far beyond getting enrolled in shipping firms or in the catering institute or some other occupation that did not demand a higher basic qualification. Children who had the inclination and resources could no doubt pursue higher studies in the nearby towns. The school management was of the opinion that vocational training should be given to the students rather than preparing them for IITs –as most of them were not interested in that. There was no plan to include higher classes when I visited the school.

This school is creating the first generation of qualified youngsters. It is only to be expected that the future generations would reach greater heights through this initiative.

They endeavour to make the students feel responsible towards their *alma mater*. Their approach is fascinating. Every classroom has an attached toilet and the ***students*** of the class would ensure that it was kept clean. This is a new experience for the children as they never had toilets in their homes in their villages.

The campus was beautiful and the students were proud of their school. Initially parent teacher meetings (PTM) witnessed chaotic scenes as the parents did not know how to conduct themselves. The ***students trained their parents*** and the PTMs became more organised.

The main aim of starting the school was to make students from the village employable adults. The ladies in-charge of the institute, were very clear in their minds about the goal that was to be achieved by the school. The catering institute in the campus ensured that the Principal and the staff were provided meals and they, instead of spending time in the kitchen in their homes, could concentrate on teaching the children even outside the school hours, if needed. Imagine how many person-hours could be saved and productively utilized this way! The Principal was provided quarters within the campus which had a kitchenette. Having provided these facilities to the Principal they expected her to coach the students who could not afford tuition fees. In short, they had planned to make the Principal on duty 24x7. And why not?

This is the only school which came close to being a "Dream School" where students, importantly those from disadvantaged background were brought to the forefront and kept in focus all the time. The infrastructure provided to them was as good as, if not better than, that provided by some elite schools.

The students were proud of their school and maintained the campus well.

After all, they owned a dream school, didn't they?

CHAPTER 20

SCHOOLS WATCH OUT!

Schools' future tense!

S ix years ago our school focused on nutritious food for children and today the same is being advocated by the government. Twenty years ago in a school, I introduced a Maths Club as a voluntary programme to make students realize that mathematics is not a drudgery but indeed fun. A Maths lab has become mandatory in some schools now. Educationists are talking about differentiated teaching and learning which was introduced by me in a school. Many websites suggest today that "Assignments by choice", "group work" and "games" are effective teaching strategies. I had experimented with these strategies in my classes twenty years ago. There was no internet at that time.

Extraordinary teachers always came out with excellent innovations which went unnoticed by the management. Such teachers continued to do good work in spite of lack of recognition from authorities. Their true judges were students. A lot of appreciation came from the student community. These days few teachers are admired by their students as dedicated and passionate teachers. This is a cause for concern.

In the age of the internet, schools, instead of reinventing the wheel, adopt the Western ways of teaching. This is good. These methods may, however, fail in Indian schools because of overcrowded class rooms, lack of infrastructure and teacher attrition. However, schools which provide the required infrastructure and training of teachers are successful in adopting the Western ways of teaching. Considering the huge student population waiting to be educated and the limited financial resources available to parents, this is a drop in the ocean.

There are schools that blindly import ideas from the net to impress the parents. On the contrary, there are schools which stubbornly refuse to accept the fact that education methods have changed in the world. They live in their own shell (or well?) refusing to even look in the direction that can bring beautiful changes in the schools that *they* have built over the years.

Fortunately, a few schools are taking a broader view of the education scenario, bringing the best of both worlds. On the basis of research about teaching in India and abroad experts are developing a vibrant curriculum. It includes a balance between the modern methods and the time tested traditional methods that best suits students of an Indian set up. This has been done keeping in view the Indian culture as the back drop. They have a vision for their schools and are not rushing with a "copy/cut and paste" job. These schools scorn rote learning and are engrossed in making education student-centric. They mean real business. The changes they are bringing about are not cosmetic. Hats off to such schools!

As far as majority of schools are concerned some dangers have already set in.

a) Teacher attrition is highest in the metros. In rural areas teacher absenteeism is the greatest drawback. It is the students who are directly affected. Retention of talented teachers is as much a challenge as finding qualified teachers.

b) More and more students are getting addicted to social networking sites. Hate messages and abuse of teachers and their peers on the sites are becoming frequent. One wonders how many schools are able to prevent this menace totally though some schools are striving to make the students aware of the dangers of these offences with limited success.

c) No code of conduct for teachers and students is in place. There are vague rules framed by the managements of schools. These are not uniformly applied to everyone.

d) Teachers are becoming increasingly vulnerable targets for students, parents and the media. Principals and management too are not spared by the media. The paranoia of these "targets" is leading to confusion and chaos in schools. In this sad state of affairs, the efficiency of running schools is hampered.

e) Students are lured by anti-social elements. Students are being subjected to drug abuse increasingly these days. Working Parents and their high profile jobs are responsible for the increasing distance between parents and their children.

f) Students come heavily under the influence of peers and therefore indulge in watching obscene stuff on TV, surfing objectionable websites, drinking, smoking and drug abuse. Violence in school buses and in schools is increasing day by day. No disciplining takes place either at home or in schools.

The definitions of right and wrong are changing continuously.

g) The high expectations of affluent parents push the students to the brink. Emotional support is as important as financial. Only the latter is provided by these parents. When the students need emotional support, they tend to rely on their peers who are too inexperienced to offer sensible advice.

h) Moral values are eroding faster than we can imagine. Parents themselves are guilty of setting bad examples. They misguide the youth by telling lies to school authorities or give misinformation. Students learn these tactics and use them on their parents. Many parents go on a denial mode if the school brings before them behavioural issues or reports the bad habits of their wards.

i) Schools and parents should understand that they both should be on the same side to correct erring children. In many instances, they get on opposite sides. Students tend to capitalise on this and escape from being corrected. Issues remain issues and are quickly forgotten due to lack of follow up. Parents may succeed in distracting school authorities but the lifelong damage that they cause to their children cannot be ignored.

j) Mal-adjusted, emotionally weak, misguided and confused students emerge out of schools which are actually meant for developing well-rounded personalities. Freedom, pocket money and lack of parental care are damaging the lives of the young school students. When they get to the college, lack of any supervision would only worsen their emotional instability. Breaking down of the joint family system is contributing to this malady in no small measure.

Schools should plan and effectively implement preventive measures to avoid untoward incidents in schools. The school staff should be oriented to keep students' safety a top priority.

How well are schools and parents prepared to tackle these issues?

CHAPTER 21

THEY MEAN
THE WORLD TO ME!

I very often reflect on what I did in various schools and how that has shaped my life. I have now retired from active involvement with schools. The intensity with which I worked in various schools as a teacher, coordinator or Principal had given me complete professional satisfaction. I had a rewarding career spanning four decades with different sets of students.

Children are wonderful everywhere—whether in Mumbai or Mundra, Jakarta or Navi Mumbai. *They* teach us many lessons which we need to learn. They are the best judges and are large hearted. I met my students who passed XII standard in 1993 in the reunion they organised in 2011. The graciousness and fondness they showed could hardly be matched by us, teachers. Students are fabulous in the way they articulate. They are guided by their true feelings and are seldom biased.

I relish and cherish the respect and affection of people with whom I have worked in many institutions.

I had, as a teacher and a Principal, made some difference to the lives of students and teachers. I did influence them in my own unique way. I cared for them and I still do.

Conducting workshops for teachers on teaching and for students on learning and having fun with maths is what I want to pursue now. In addition I attend workshops and seminars on student-specific issues so that I understand students of this generation better. I read about schools and education to keep myself up-to-date on the subject.

Teaching is the only profession where one is in constant touch with the young generation. A teacher, who is passionate about her profession, can make a significant impact on school going kids.

I want to be in touch with children.

Because they mean the world to me.

ANNEX

The following pages provide a compilation of some of the articles relating to school education which were submitted by Mrs.Vimala Nandakumar to DNA Navi Mumbai. The articles were published with the editor's touch on the dates indicated against each article:

Shocking Incident!

The recent incident of a student stabbing his teacher in Chennai sent shock waves across the country. Both the families-of the teacher and the student will take time to come to terms with the tragic event. The children of the teacher have lost their mother at such a tender age. No one can replace the mother of the children. The teacher was only doing her duty as a teacher. On the other hand we need to sympathise with the student who has got into a mess in such early stage in life. If only he had learnt to manage his anger and frustration, he would have been attending school like his peers now.

This reflects the kind of upbringing children have these days. It is true parents bring up their children differently these days unlike our days. The worst critic in our days were our mothers. They passed hurting remarks at our dresses, behaviour or way of talking. For ever we were criticised in front of guests and pulled up for our shortcomings of any sort. We were bullied by our cousins and occasional encouragement came from uncles or aunts who visited us. We grew up among siblings learning vital lessons on denial and sacrifice. No or very less importance was given to our likes and dislikes. All that parents provided us was food and decent clothing. Parents thought we could become arrogant if a word of praise for our good grades or behaviour came our way. Comparisons with peers or siblings were common. We learnt to be emotionally tough from early days. We had no other choice. We handled failure by swallowing the pain that came along with it and secretly enjoyed success.

Now a days we find most families having either one child or two children. This has resulted in children being denied of many tough lessons of life. We hardly enjoyed any luxuries when we were young but the current generation can hardly take "no" from parents. They are intolerant to any kind of remarks or criticism from any one. With family support vanishing children have no one to turn to. Their peers do not offer much help and teachers tend to be judgemental sometimes. Conflicts in schools are taken seriously that parents get summoned often to parents-teacher meetings. This stresses the children because both the parents need to take a day off to attend to these meetings. Children lie in order to avoid any arguments with parents. Parents saying that their children share every secret with them should be taken with a pinch of salt.

Schools are being more and more challenged with behavioural problems of children. With very little cooperation coming from parents, teachers are bound to be faced with aggressive behaviour of students in future. Failing in an exam or rustication is unheard off these days for the fear of losing the child. Children resort to extreme steps and school teachers become easy targets.

Parents need to spend unstructured time with their children. Mothers or fathers need to give up some of the outings or TV programmes and cancel innumerable classes(tuitions, grammar, Bollywood dance etc) where they have enrolled their children. They should spend some quality time with the children teaching them how wonderful and precious life is and more importantly how to enjoy life.

Published under the title "Give kids attention" on 22 Feb 2012.

No-fail policy

A news report about grace marks being awarded to failed students of standard IX is very disturbing. Such Government directives are unduly strengthening the hands of the parents as well as the students. Some teachers will be tempted to take teaching lightly due to such policies. Some may feel frustrated and lose interest in teaching.

If students are not going to be detained till std VIII what will motivate them to learn? Why would a parent not take the child for vacations during school days if they are assured that the child will get promoted to the next class? What will ensure that teaching quality will not get affected in classes if the teacher knows that no child will be detained?

Curriculum is about "what to teach", "how to teach" and "whether teaching was done". Tests and exams not only put pressure on students to learn and perform well but also are evaluation tools to check if learning has been effectively facilitated by the teachers in class rooms. It is important that students take learning and teachers take teaching seriously. There are already increasing cases of students bunking classes, smoking, drug abuse, misusing Facebook, threatening teachers and in some cases getting into bad company. (A teacher was stabbed to death in Chennai and a principal slapped by a student in Mumbai recently)

It is true that a few students come under terrible pressure to perform well in exams failing which they resort to extreme steps. The parents have to be educated and made aware the *dangers of pushing their children to perform well. There should be debates, workshops and seminars on various aspects that cause stress to students. Making life easy for them by introducing such policies will only weaken the education system. This is a dangerous move.*

Introduction of no-fail policy will affect the quality of students passing out of schools. It is these children who will end up being unemployable adults later in their lives. What are we doing by interfering with the education system which brought India a prominent place on the global map?

The authority of principals and teachers are weakened by the introduction of "no fail policy till Standard VIII" or "grace marks for failed students" or "making external exams for std X optional. "Are we not creating a Frankenstein's Monster?

Published under the title "No fail policy might affect quality of teaching" on 22, May 2012

Fire safety!

Fire at Mantralaya! Unbelievable indeed! The head quarters of state government, place where officials ruling the state sit got engulfed by fire last week. This is not some slum where such incidents take place due to carelessness on the part of dwellers but the very building where safety of not only concerned officials running the state should have been top priority but also important files concerning the State. If it was callousness of authorities concerned then it cannot be brushed aside and if the cause is sabotage then the story is quite a different topic of debate.

If the fire safety norms had been ignored then some drastic measures should be implemented immediately. We are not talking of Mantralaya alone. Many buildings and schools are prone to fire accidents. In case of some disaster or terrorist striking a school, are the school authorities in a state of preparedness to tackle them?

Some schools, I have observed are not at all safe for the children and the staff.

a)   There is just one staircase leading to the upper floors. In case of a fire accident on the ground floor or any of the lower floors there can be no escape route available for the children and staff on the higher floors.

b)   Catering services are offered to students and staff in many schools these days. Generally the kitchen is on the ground floor. Students and staff will get trapped on the higher floors in case of a blast of the gas cylinder/s in the kitchen.

c) *No fire drills are conducted in schools regularly. These should be done at least twice a year. A safe place needs to be identified near the school building so that the children and staff can assemble there in case of a fire accident. Many schools are in residential areas where there is hardly any place for students even to play. In case of an emergency where will the children assemble?*

d) *Are the concerned authorities aware of the fact that first the elevators will stop working in such cases?*

e) *Are the authorities running the schools aware of the fact that disabled persons need to be physically brought down to a safe place on the ground floor?*

In a school I worked abroad fire mock drills were conducted twice a year.

- *A safe place was identified near the school and students were instructed to move to that place quickly in a line without panicking. (They were advised to leave their belongings in the class rooms.) The fire alarm went off and the bursar clocked the time taken by the students and the staff to evacuate the entire building.*

- *The alarms were set off on another day (without informing the students) so that the students would follow all the instructions that were given to them earlier during the mock drill. The time was again recorded.(Since the planning and execution was done well, the clocked time was much less than that of the first drill)*

- *Two students were identified to lift a physically challenged boy to the ground floor during the drill.*
- *The attendance lists were always kept at the reception on the ground floor so that the class teachers picked them up and rushed to the safe place to check if she had all her class students safely assembled at the designated place.*

I don't know how many schools undertake these precautions, whether they are serious, whether they have space or programme about introducing these measures to protect lives of children of the schools. Do they really care or just making school a profitable business venture? Were the provisions of these safety measures taken into consideration when they were given permission to start the school? Are parents themselves aware of these considerations?

If Mantralaya has not had systems in place what can one say about the other places in the state? Ours is a country where pizzas arrive faster than fire engines. It is a shame that we do not care for children-the future of the country.

Are we hoping that nothing untoward will happen to our children in schools or are we sitting on a time bomb?

Published under the title "Are schools ready to combat fire" on 3, July 2012

Right To Education Act

Any law that is made by the government is opposed vehemently. Otherwise loopholes in them are discovered by people to escape complying with them. In most of the cases, the rules are flouted royally because of lack of research undertaken by the government before promulgating the law or absence of clear guidelines for implementing the law.

One such law is RTE –reservation of 25% of seats for the under-privileged children in schools. The talk has been there about such provision towards slum children for quite some time. It is a noble thought indeed but why introduce vagueness in the law? Why can't the government plug all the loop holes so that the act gets implemented without any hurdle?

Here are some points to ponder:

a) *Government is aware or should be aware of the fact that the admissions in schools close by December every year. Schools vie with each other to capture prospective "clients", namely, the students to collect fees much in advance. Hence schools are now saying that they can implement this rule only next year.*

b) *Next, why exempt Ved Pathshalas and Madarsas from the RTE act initially and then extend the exemption to schools with minority status? Now all schools have jumped into the minority band wagon saying they cannot admit slum children as they have minority status.*

This defeats the very purpose of the RTE rule.

c) *Why not stick to the June 11, 2012 dead line for admission of under-privileged students so that schools take the act seriously? By extending the date of admission of, the government is only ensuring that some of the 25% reserved seats remain vacant which could have been allotted to other students.*

d) *Is it possible, as claimed by certain section of people, that the potential beneficiaries of the act were not aware of this act? If that is the case why did the government not create awareness among people of the slums? This should have been done right from the day the rule was being formulated.*

e) *There is no clarity about the cost incurred by the schools in educating these 25% children. Should the other parents bear the cost of educating the 25%? They are already burdened with the fees they have to pay for their own children. Is the government going to take the entire responsibility? How can the schools pay their staff and also include the cost of providing education for the 25% children?*

It appears that government is not serious about this act and the schools are looking for excuses to escape implementing the same. Who is the loser in the whole exercise? The poor children, of course! It is a case of double whammy for them because they are tempted with this offer which is not going to materialise in good measure.

All this defeats the very purpose of the introduction of the RTE act.

Published under the title "RTE: Govt unsure, schools search for escape route" on 19 June 2012

Why this Kolaveri over Exams di?

The examination fever of the students of Standard X and Standard XII has affected not only principals, teachers and parents but also other people. Those of us who have no children appearing for these exams are anxious to read the news paper for articles on what is happening to students all over the city.

Eating and sleeping disorders of students worry parents who are relying on tips from professionals whereas principals and teachers are anxious about their students' performances and the results. Students who should be relaxed at the time of examination are stressed out. Students, in this crucial year, have sacrificed entertainment of all sorts and spent all their precious time in school and coaching classes. One would expect them to perform well in the exams. Why then this unexplainable tension? Is it the worry about getting a seat in a good college or falling short of parents' expectations or their own? Peer pressure? Evaluation of their answer sheets?

Some suggestions to ease the tension at least for the future batch of students:

a) *Schools need to reduce the **class strength** to 25 or maximum of 30. The teaching will lack quality and effectiveness if the number extends to 60 to 75 as is the case with many schools.*

b) *Have **more examiners** and pay them well. Do not expect examiners to correct 500 papers in ten days. The quality of correction of papers will suffer.*

Every school should send its teachers (proportional to the students they send for Std X and Std XII) for correction of answer scripts. This should be made compulsory irrespective of whether the school is private or govt-aided. The marks of these exams decide the future of students. Can we afford to be callous about this?

c) *Parents should not make a big fuss about these exams and push their children to perform well. They have ensured that things left undone by schools are taken care of by enrolling their children in coaching classes. They have done their **duty as parents** well and should relax during the exams.*

d) *Students should believe in themselves and their abilities. This period is like slog overs of an ODI cricket match. They are sure to **win**.*

Published under the title "Board exams are over rated" on 11 March 2012